HONKY TONKIN'

A TRAVEL GUIDE TO AMERICAN MUSIC

"There's a war going on. The enemy is fast-food, Interstates, non-dairy creamer, *People* magazine and 90% of what's on the radio. The Liberation Army is me and my friends, and our best weapons are cayenne, garlic and regional music. There're a lot of us scattered across the country — we share a passion for old music, vanishing lifestyles, concrete history. Music is a big part but food is just as important. Also beer, hats, drinking, hot sauce, barnside graphics, railroad trains, gospel churches and clowns. As often as my work lets me, I go road-running to see how the battle is raging — check my friends to see what they've turned up, look to see that some of the old stuff is still alive, hear some music, eat some food, go honky tonkin'."

Michael Goodwin, **Village Voice**

"A lot of people would agree that rock and roll has gone to the disco dogs and the LA plastic mellow fellows. It's all beginning to sound the same, but worse than that, it's begun to sound meaningless. Artists and groups are now being 'marketed' like paper towels, tight playlists rule the radio, and records are referred to as 'product' within the industry. Lawyers, accountants and financial people run most of the labels instead of the seat-of-the-pants music pioneers of old. However a discerning listener can still discover real music in this vast abyss of plastic nothingness."

John Lomax, **Rock 'n' New Mania and the Boogie Woogie News**

HONKY TONKIN'

A TRAVEL GUIDE TO AMERICAN MUSIC

BY RICHARD WOOTTON

Honky Tonkin': A Travel Guide to American Music
Third British Edition, First American Edition

Published in Britain by
Travelaid Publishing
P.O. Box 369
London NW3 4ER
Telephone (0403) 731174
Telex 87493

ISBN 0 902743 16 3

Published in the United States of America by
The East Woods Press
820 East Boulevard
Charlotte, North Carolina 28203
Telephone (704) 334-0897

ISBN 0-914788-26-4
Library of Congress No. 80-503

Printed in the United States of America
by the George Banta Company.
Typography by Raven Type.

CONTENTS

HONKY TONKIN'

A TRAVEL GUIDE TO
AMERICAN MUSIC

INTRODUCTION

This book is, I hope, reasonably straightforward. It's intended for anyone seeking good music in America, both live and on record — more than just top-40 pop. It will guide you to older music forms that are at the roots of today's rock and roll: from blues which is still alive and flourishing in Chicago to regional music that's survived relatively unchanged for many years; from Cajun music in the French areas of Louisiana to non-commercial genres; from bluegrass to the newest rock sounds emerging from the arid wastelands of Cleveland, Ohio, as well as the chic cities of New York and Los Angeles.

On arrival in one of the big American cities you should have little trouble finding the local Fillmore, Civic Auditoriums, Astrodomes and other major nightspots. Concerts at these places are usually well advertised in local papers and magazines. It's the smaller spots, especially clubs, that can pose the problems, and much of the best music emanates from these places. A large part of the listings for the big towns and cities is therefore taken up with information on clubs that feature interesting live music.

The information published in this book was, as far as possible, correct at the time of going to press. However we can accept no liability for errors, omissions or changes. Musicians and club owners tend to lead complicated lives and it's always advisable to check by phone before you go anywhere. Some clubs require proof of your age and you may be asked to show your ID. Foreign visitors who look young are advised to carry their passports with them.

This guide couldn't have been compiled without the generous contributions of a large number of people. I won't be able to do another one unless I can get feedback from those who use this edition. I'd be very grateful for any help — there are forms at the back of the book for additions and corrections. Clippings from magazines and newspapers have proved especially useful in the past.

Richard Wootton

United States

# of America

CANADA
LAKE SUPERIOR
MINNESOTA
LAKE HURON
MICHIGAN
ST. LAWRENCE RIVER
MAINE
VERMONT
NEW HAMPSHIRE
LAKE ONTARIO
NEW YORK
CAMBRIDGE
BOSTON
MASS
CONN
RHODE ISLAND
WISCONSIN
MINNEAPOLIS
ST. PAUL
LAKE MICHIGAN
MILWAUKEE
DETROIT
LAKE ERIE
NEW YORK
IOWA
OMAHA
CHICAGO
INDIANA
CLEVELAND
AKRON
COLUMBUS
PENNSYLVANIA
NEW JERSEY
PHILADELPHIA
DELAWARE
MARYLAND
ILLINOIS
INDIANAPOLIS
OHIO
WASHINGTON D.C.
WEST VIRGINIA
VIRGINIA
KANSAS CITY
ST. LOUIS
MISSOURI
KENTUCKY
NORTH CAROLINA
NASHVILLE
TENNESSEE
MEMPHIS
TULSA
ATLANTIC OCEAN
ARKANSAS
ATLANTA
SOUTH CAROLINA
CHARLESTON
MACON
ALABAMA
GEORGIA
MISSISSIPPI
LOUISIANA
HOUSTON
NEW ORLEANS
GULF OF MEXICO
FLORIDA
BAHAMA ISLANDS
MIAMI
0 100 200 300 400 500 miles

ATLANTA, GEORGIA

Home of Coca-Cola, national leader in the production of processed chicken, one of the few cities of the world not on a navigable river, capital of Jimmy Carter's home state of Georgia and the place that most dramatically expresses the transition from the old to the new South that he is associated with — tree-lined residential streets where magnolia and dogwood trees surround Georgian mansions are only a short distance from the dazzling new office blocks of glass and steel — Atlanta is a great place for live music both on a national and local level.

Atlanta, and nearby Macon, have produced some of the most creative musicians in popular music. R&B greats like Otis Redding, James Brown, Ray Charles, Chuck Willis, Clarence Carter and Little Richard have been associated with these environs. Pop stars like Joe South, Tommy Roe and Billy Joe Royal gained success through an association with the local 'song factory', Lowery Music, and in the seventies Capricorn Records was at the forefront of the progressive rock movement of the South with the Allman Brothers Band and the Marshall Tucker Band.

Little Feat's "Oh Atlanta" has a line that goes, "You can drop me off on Peachtree," and refers to the street that runs from the middle of town into the suburbs. Several clubs can be found along this road. The Hotel Georgian Terrace at 659 Peachtree (Tel: 872-6671) is a funky establishment that's cheap but clean and recommended as a good base for musical visitors as it's close to three of the best nightspots — The Fox is across the street, Rose's Cantina is two blocks west and The Agora is in the same building.

Downtown Atlanta is all black these days except for white pockets that are convention centers or special tourist areas like the Omni, "a Playboy dream without the sex," and Underground Atlanta. The Omni at 100 Techwood Drive Viaduct is a gigantic megastructure of shops, restaurants, hotels, an amazing skating rink, and a large hall that's home to the Atlanta Hawks Basketball and Atlanta Flames Ice Hockey teams and showplace for major rock acts like Fleetwood Mac. Concert capacity here is over 16,000.

Underground Atlanta is on Central Avenue near Alabama Street and consists of four blocks of subterranean structures that have been restored to "their 1890s glory" with shops, restaurants and clubs. Underground Atlanta has certainly seen better days since it opened in 1969, and although worth a short visit, it is by no means essential. There are several clubs, many with free admission, featuring bands with some high caliber musicians wasting their talent playing top-40 tunes. Three clubs with more original music are Muhlenbrink's Saloon, Scarlett O'Hara's and Dante's Down The Hatch.

The best guide to what's on is the *Atlanta Gazette*, a weekly paper that has a detailed and helpful guide to the best live music plus a "Honky Tonks" listing in the "Week at a Glance" section. *Southern Jam* is a freebie that covers the local music scene. *Creative Loafing* is another free paper covering the arts in general and has some music pieces. The *Atlanta Journal-Constitution* has a useful "Week Ahead" guide each Saturday morning.

CONCERT HALLS AND CLUBS

The Fox, 660 Peachtree, 881-1977.
Magnificent place that's highly recommended for almost any concert because the interior is so attractive and the acoustics are excellent. The second largest movie theater in America (Radio City in New York is the biggest), it's a genuine piece of American escapism from the thirties in kitsch Moorish and Egyptian style. 3000 capacity.

Agora Ballroom, 665 Peachtree, 87A-GORA. Purpose-built rock club modeled on the successful Ohio nightspots of the same name. Its main floor and balconies afford visibility for 1300 people and a 74-foot bar with computerized stations keeps the crowds tanked-up most nights. Big names in rock, jazz and disco. The Agora was built on the site of Alex Cooley's Electric Ballroom, a popular Atlanta nightspot for many years.

Great Southeast Music Hall, Cherokee Plaza (north on Peachtree). This club moved in 1978 from its Broadview Plaza location that was the scene of the first American appearance by the Sex Pistols. Most acts that play here are national names with a country or folk flavor. The walls feature autographs of past performers, though no new artists can be persuaded to sign the largely empty section that has the signatures of Ronnie Van Zandt and Jim Croce who've since died in tragic accidents.

Rose's Cantina, 688 Spring St., at 3rd St., 881-0244. On a good night — and this place has many, especially at weekends — this can be one of the best nightspots in town for good-time, sweat-soaked music from the likes of Delbert McClinton, local hero Glenn Phillips, The Nighthawks from Washington, DC and rockers like The Para Band.

Muhlenbrink's Saloon, Underground Atlanta, 525-8495. Bluesman Piano Red plays short sets here each night between longer sets by a competent bluegrass band. Willie Lee Perryman, aka Piano Red and Dr. Feelgood, is an albino barrelhouse pianist best known for his recordings of "Right String But the Wrong Yo-Yo" and "Dr. Feelgood."

Scarlett O'Hara's, Underground Atlanta. Features well known soul bands from the past like The Drifters and Chairman of the Board.

Dante's Down the Hatch, Underground Atlanta, 577-1800. Take the wooden steps down below street level and you'll find the replica of an old ship at dock. You can choose between folk music at the dock side or jazz on board ship.

C.W. Shaw's, 4166 Buford Highway, 634-6757. One of the few club owners in America with a master's degree in law, Chuck Rinaldo is proud to have one of the best sound systems in Atlanta. Local rock bands on the up and up are featured. The club has a history of famous names dropping by unexpectedly and sitting in.

Downtown Cafe, corner of Virginia and Highland, 875-7709. A funky little room with a bar and good vegetarian food. Regular acts here include Yikes!, a funky light jazz group; The Band of Desperate Men, an eclectic collection of jazz, blues, rock and oldies; and blues slide-guitarist Eilen McIllwaine.

HONKY TONKIN'

The Peanut Palace, on the square of McDonough (about 40 minutes drive from Atlanta — phone them on 957-5454 and ask for directions). Rock spot in a 1930s picture palace where the seats have been removed.

RECORD STORE

Wax and Fax, Little Five Points, 423 Moreland Ave., NE Atlanta. Three miles from downtown, this store specializes in used records (from $2) and music books. Owner Don Baird is very helpful and will do his best to get you those hard-to-get items you've been looking for over the years.

Macon, Georgia

Eighty-five miles down the Interstate from Atlanta is Macon, the town where Little Richard was born in 1932, James Brown was discovered, Otis Redding was launched as a performer, and the Allman Brothers Band members call home. Macon is sleepy-eyed and typically old-time South, full of magnolias and dogwoods. The Greyhound bus station is where rock 'n' roll star Little Richard (plain Richard Penniman then) used to wash dishes and wrote "Tutti Frutti." Soul singer James Brown got his start here as a teenager with The Famous Flames at the Two-Spot bar on 5th Street — he's still remembered by many people in town including the popular DJ Hamp Swain who's still broadcasting on the local black station WIBB 1280am. Otis Redding was at high school here and was so impressed with the adulation showered on Little Richard that he decided to become a full-time performer with the aid of his friend and future manager Phil Walden. After Otis' untimely death (the Otis Redding Bridge over Macon's Ocmulgee River is dedicated to his memory), Walden went on to discover The Allman Brothers Band and launch them to fame and fortune through his own Capricorn label. Duanne Allman and Berry Oakley, two of the founder members of the Allman Brothers Band, are buried in Rose Hill Cemetery where the band used to relax in the predawn darkness after rehearsals.

CLUBS

Grant's Lounge, 576 Poplar St., 746-7671. Rock and soul.

Banana's (formerly Uncle Sam's), 2211 Gray Highway, 742-1492. Country music.

New Directions, 533 3rd St., 745-3091. Disco and soul.

(Special thanks to *Tony Paris*)

BOSTON, MASSACHUSETTS

For a city so small — Boston and Cambridge combined have a population of only about 750,000 — there is a great deal of good music available in a variety of styles. Only New York and Los Angeles, both of which are 10 times Boston's size, can compare with this city for musical diversity on the local level. There are several large places to accommodate the frequent big name rock concerts, and a large number of radio stations broadcasting music — with WCAS and WBCN seeming to have the edge over the others. The record collector won't be disappointed in Boston and European visitors will be pleased to find many albums, considered rare at home, easily obtainable at reasonable prices.

The economy of much of the local music scene is directly related to the purchasing power of the students on the several campuses in the Boston/Cambridge area, and the long summer months are usually a quiet time of the year. Boston clubs tend to be expensive — if you want to have a good time without spending too much money check out the Cambridge coffee houses in the area around Harvard Square.

Boston is a great pedestrian town, which means that if your budget doesn't run to hiring a car you needn't be too restricted in getting around. The city seems very popular with both foreign and domestic tourists alike, and is also a favorite for conventions. All this results in critical accommodation shortages at times and, even in winter, major hotels can be booked up several weeks in advance.

Rock bands in Boston come and go with great frequency either heading off to national fame and fortune — like The Cars and Boston — or disintegrating after a few months. But three long-established acts — a blues band and two modern country outfits — have been delighting the patrons of Boston clubs for many years and deserve to be mentioned as they're little known outside New England. Chuck McDermott and his band are talented country-rock musicians who're handicapped outside their home base because people are conditioned to expect good new country acts to come only from the South. John Lincoln Wright and his Sour Mash Boys play country music that's more rooted in old-timey styles but with a modern feel.

Roomful of Blues, a seven-man band from Rhode Island who perform highly-charged recreations of forties rhythm and blues, and jazz tunes, have built up a strong following on the club circuit between Boston and Rhode Island in the same manner as The Nighthawks and The Allstars in the Washington area, George Thorogood and the Destroyers in Delaware and The Fabulous Thunderbirds in Texas. All these outfits are made up of white musicians keeping alive blues and R&B traditions.

Big name rock acts usually appear at the Orpheum, Boston Garden, Music Hall or the Berklee Performance Center. The area has many clubs and bars featuring live music — this selection includes most of the best. For up-to-date information about clubs and who's playing where, check either of the two weekly papers, *The Boston Phoenix* with its "Boston After Dark" section or *The Boston Real Paper.*

BOSTON CLUBS

The Rat, 528 Commonwealth Ave., 247-7713. Important breeding ground for Boston and New York new wave rock bands. Music here seven nights a week with the cover varying with the group. The album "Live At The Rat" featured 10 local punk bands on the club's own Rat label.

Cantone's, 69 Broad St., 338-7677. Another new wave nightspot.

Lulu White, 3 Appleton St., off Copley Sq., 423-3652. Jazz supper club with name attractions, Tues.-Thurs.

Club 76, 76 Batterymarch St., 524-3377. According to *The Real Paper*, "A place for women and their friends. Disco on Fri. and Sat., entertainment on Thurs. and Sun. Women visual arts exhibit monthly."

HONKY TONKIN'

Michael's, 52A Gainsboro St., 247-7262. Live jazz every night. Local musicians perform in relaxed atmosphere. Cover $1.

Pooh's, 464 Commonwealth Ave., 262-6911. The back room here has some of the finest jazz in Boston in the best possible setting.

Sword In The Stone, 13 Charles St., 523-9168. Boston's oldest intimate coffee house featuring finest local artists nightly. Open hoots Tues. and Sun.

The Paradise, 967 Commonwealth Ave., 254-2052. Live music nightly in this large club. Mostly top acts with prices varying according to the artist. Diverse musical policy, ranging from blues and jazz to new wave rock.

CAMBRIDGE CLUBS

Speakeasy, 24 Norfolk near Central Sq., 661-9887. The only club in the Boston area to feature live blues seven nights a week.

Jonathan Swift's, 30 Boylston St., Harvard Sq. Live folk or rock most nights. Geoff Muldaur, John Hammond recently.

Back Room At The Idler, 123 Mt. Aubern Sq., 354-9489. Remember when coffee houses were underground, dark and smoky? This place even has real bricks. Music free and often very good but the booze is expensive.

Inn Square Men's Bar, 1350 Cambridge St., 354-8454. Don't believe the name — there are women here too. A crazy atmosphere thanks to the zany tastes of the owners. You're never quite sure what you'll find except the "dancing turkey sandwich."

1369 Club, 1369 Cambridge St., Inman Sq. Live jazz seven nights a week, no cover. Nice friendly atmosphere to listen to good jazz. Happy hour 'til 9.

Cantab Lounge, 738 Massachusetts Ave., in Central Sq. Country, folk and blues.

Passim, 47 Palmer St., Harvard Sq., 492-7679. Best live folk in the city. Local and name acts. Live show from here on WCAS 740AM Suns., 2 to 4 PM.

Jacks, 952 Massachusetts Ave., 491-7800. Popular club where Bonnie Raitt was once a regular.

Oxford Ale House, 36 Church St., Harvard Sq., 876-5353. Popular club featuring local rock and roll bands.

RECORD SHOPS

The Coop and **Music City** are recommended big stores with branches in Boston and Cambridge. **Cheapo Records** in Central Square (next to the Post Office) sells most records for less than $2. **Deja Vu** has two shops that sell a lot of oldies — 151 Massachusetts Ave. in Boston and 1105 Massachusets Ave. in Cambridge.

Skippy White's The Original Oldies But Goodies Land, mentioned in previous editions of this guide, has moved to 257 Huntington Ave., Boston (beside the Symphony Hall), 262-4545. They claim to have "the largest inventory of oldies on 45 in New England" — more than a quarter million. They buy and sell used records.

Zoundz, 845 Boylston St., Boston, 267-2555. Recommended for second-hand records and cheap copies of new releases. There's a restaurant below this store with a wide range of good food at modest prices if you want a break from going through the vinyl goodies.

RADIO

WCAS 740AM is recommended. They play a lot of music on small labels like Flying Fish. **WBCN FM** is a highly respected station that plays a wide range of music: rock, jazz and blues.

(Special thanks to *Barry Ballard*)

CHICAGO, ILLINOIS

Chicago has a rich and varied music scene, is renowned as the center of the blues world, boasts the strongest folk music scene in America and has an impressive amount of local jazz activity. A visit is recommended, especially if you have friends or relatives who can show you around. People traveling on their own should take care, because parts of this city are very dangerous. As with New York, never look lost, innocent or naive — even if you are.

America's second largest city stretches over 25 miles along Lake Michigan. The view from a boat on the lake is breathtaking — the center of Chicago has some of the most impressive examples of modern architecture you'll ever see. I always thought big buildings were ugly until I came here.

There are clubs and bars featuring live music throughout the city and its suburbs, but if you're on your own without a car and making only a brief visit you'd be well advised to base yourself in the North Lincoln area. This is one of the safer parts of town and has several clubs, cheap eating houses and hotels nearby. Good blues, jazz and folk can be heard within a few blocks.

Big name rock acts play the International Amphitheater at 43rd and Halstead; Chicago Stadium, 1800 W. Madison (the sound is said to be poor at both places); the 4000-seat Auditorium Theater at 70 E. Congress ("Comfy seats and good sound"); The Aragon Ballroom, 1106 W. Lawrence Ave.; The Uptown Theater, 4816 N. Broadway; and The Riviera Theater, 4746 N. Racine.

Chicago has had a strong folk music tradition for years and Steve Goodman, Bonnie Kolac, John Prine and Jim Post are probably the best known artists associated with it. The golden days when there were over a dozen good clubs and scores of fine singers are long gone. Economics caught up with many of the small folk clubs, and competition from Park West and the medium-sized concert halls has led to nightspots closing or changing policy. Earl Pionke, who owns two of the best clubs, The Earl of Old Town and Somebody Else's Troubles, has had to cut back on live bookings during the week. Nevertheless, weekends offer a rich choice of folk music and there are still enough spots and good singers to ensure Chicago remains as America's folk capital.

Folk music enthusiasts should check the weekly *Reader* for club listings, call or visit the Folklore Society Center, 907 W. Armitage, 528-1818, for specific enquiries, and listen to "Midnight Special" on WFMT 98.7FM or 1340AM on a Saturday night at 10:15PM (repeated Wednesday afternoons at 1:00PM). This is a "crazy three-hour quilt of traditional music from the Americas and abroad, comedy, and recordings of Chicago locals singing in the clubs." It's one of the most famous radio programs in the US and has done a lot to keep folk consciousness alive in the area.

There's a fair amount of jazz activity in Chicago. The Jazz Institute of Chicago, based at Rick's Cafe American — an excellent nightspot at the Lakeshore Holiday Inn, has become quite a force in jazz of late and maintains a hotline — (313) 666-1881 — which has a taped announcement of most jazz activity in the city.

There are several country music places in the Chicago suburbs, but I'm reluctant to recommend many. While it's the *area* around some blues clubs that are dangerous, some of the clubs that feature country and rockabilly are themselves dangerous, and you'd be unwise to go with less than four people.

Downtown Chicago is called "The Loop" on account of the elevated train tracks that loop around this central district. The trains are easily the noisiest to be found anywhere in the States — conversation is almost impossible — but they have an unforgetable charm. Within the five- by seven-block area of The Loop there are many interesting shops, including good bookstores and some large record shops with cut-out racks. During the summer months, free lunchtime entertainment is available in this area — most notably at Richard J. Daley Plaza, Washington and Clark; First National Bank Plaza, Monroe and Clark; and Pioneer Court, Michigan

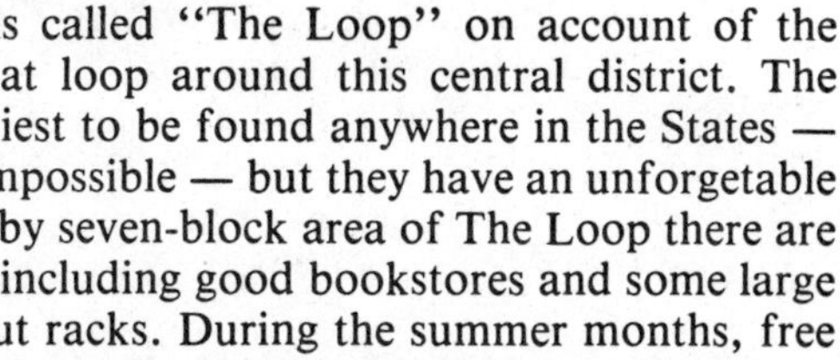

Ave., at the Chicago River. Listings can be found in the daily papers.

The best guide to gigs is the *Reader*, an excellent free weekly paper that is published each Friday and is available from an assortment of book stores, record shops, bars and restaurants. *Illinois Entertainer* is a monthly paper that lists gigs throughout the state. *Triad* is a bi-monthly music paper that's sponsored by a local radio station. WXRT 93FM has a program "This Week In Chicago" every Monday night at 10PM that features the artists appearing in town in the coming week.

CLUBS

Park West, 322 W. Armitage, 929-5959. Showcase club that gets great artists and is probably the best place in town sight and sound wise, but is expensive.

The Quiet Knight, 953 W. Belmont, 348-7100. Once the city's most beloved folk club and the place where Steve Goodman met Arlo Guthrie, it now has an unpredictable booking policy with jazz, folk, blues and rock of variable quality. On a good night there are few better places to be — like Saturday, July 10, 1978 when Muddy Waters was joined on stage for an impromptu jam session by Mick Jagger and three other Rolling Stones along with Willie Dixon.

B. Ginnings, 1227 E. Golf Rd., Schaumburg, 882-8484. Fashionable rock club, with nationally known performers, owned by the drummer with the successful rock outfit Chicago, Danny Seraphine.

Orphan's, 2462 N. Lincoln, 929-2677. The back room at Orphan's provides a varied fare of music with good sound at reasonable prices. Blues, jazz or folk every night of the week.

Wise Fools Pub, 2270 N. Lincoln, 929-1510. Popular, crowded club. Rock, jazz and folk occasionally, but blues is the most frequently featured music.

Clearwater Saloon, 3447 N. Lincoln, 935-6545. No cover and no minimum. Folk, country and occasional jazz. Good music in a comfortable atmosphere.

Biddy Mulligan's, 7644 N. Sheridan. 761-6532. Singles bar with frequent blues artists.

Earl of Old Town, 1615 N. Wells, 642-5206. The launching pad for Steve Goodman, John Prine and Bonnie Koloc and the place where they still make occasional appearances. Live folk every night of the week. Monday is "Open Hoot," Tuesdays are workshops nights, Wednesdays and Thursdays feature traditional music and the weekends are reserved for name performers. It should be noted that at most Chicago folk spots, people take the music very seriously and it's a case of "sit down and shut up" when singers are on stage.

Somebody Else's Troubles, 2470 N. Lincoln, 929-0660. While The Earl has been home to the bigger names, this club has long been a center for the lesser-known Chicago singer-songwriters and for traditional music. Live music is now restricted to weekends — local talent like Mike and Barbara Smith, new acts, and folkies from the surrounding states.

Old Town School of Folk Music, 909 W. Armitage, 525-7472. Refuge for traditional music and a place where the emphasis is on participation. There is another Old Town School in Evanstown at 927 Noyes, 525-7793.

Barbarossa, 1117 N. Dearborn, 751-0624. According to *Chicago* magazine, "If business picks up, they just might be able to repair and repaint this crumbling but friendly Near-North Bar — it's the only place an aspiring young folk act can get a start. Music and drink flow until 4AM." Open mike on Tuesdays, well known Chicago singer/songwriters at weekends.

Charlotte's Web, 728 First Ave., Rockford, (815) 965-8933. Located in a former synagogue built in 1917, this comfortable club devoted to music, mostly folk, is highly recommended by customers and musicians alike. Excellent sound. (Rockford, Illinois, is about 60 miles from Chicago.)

Jazz Showcase, 901 N. Rush, 337-1000. Excellent music from top names. Three sets a night at 9, 11 and 1.

Rick's Cafe American, Holiday Inn, 644 N. Lake Shore Dr., 943-9200. A delightful jazz spot with top flight performers, an intimate, informal atmosphere and a design that recalls the club run by Humphrey Bogart as Rick in the movie "Casablanca."

Redford's, 2548 N. Halsted, 549-1250. Name artists at the weekend, local talent — with no cover charge — during the week.

Backroom, 1007 N. Rush, 944-2132. Intimate jazz club.

Colette's, 2515 N. Lincoln, 477-5022. Jazz every night in popular North Lincoln nightspot.

Gaspars, 3159 N. Southport, 871-6680. Name jazz and blues talent.

Country Music Inn, Milwaukee Ave. and Aptastic Road, Prairie View, 541-7670. Traditional country place with black lights, square-tiled dance floor and plenty of cowgirls to two-step the night away. The band Western Echoes plays from Wednesdays through Sundays. Neither Country Music Inn nor Nashville North (see below) fall into the category of dangerous country music places mentioned above!

Nashville North, 101 E. Irving Pk., Bensenville, 595-0170. Probably the best club for country music in the area — large, friendly with good sound and food. Dave Gibson and Hackenbush, a bunch of highly competent musicians, are the house band here.

RECORD SHOPS

Old Town Folklore Center, 907 W. Armitage, 528-1818. Sells instruments, books and records, including independently produced albums by Chicago's own, that you'll have difficulty finding elsewhere.

Rolling Stone, 175 W. Washington and La Salle (subway Washington), 346-3489. Downtown in The Loop. Hundreds of cutouts at cheap prices.

Rose Records, 214 S. Wabash, 939-9542. Good for out-of-print items. Records grouped according to labels rather than artists or musical genre, which can make finding a specific record difficult unless you're a knowledgeable collector.

Sounds Good, 4821 W. Irving Park; 3176 N. Broadway; 3259 N. Ashland Ave. Three good stores in the same chain.

Laury's Discount Records, 201 La Salle, 263-3023.

RADIO

There are over 50 AM and FM stations broadcasting in the Chicago area and their wavelengths can be found in the daily papers. Probably the best progressive rock station is WXRT 93 FM. It has a good mixture of musical styles, simulcasts some public TV rock shows and occasional live shows. The station has some good DJs including a lady called Terri Hummert who has forgotten more about popular music that most of us will ever know, and the bizarre Scott McConnell. WBEZ 91.5 FM has a Jazz Forum every night at 9PM and Folk Festival USA is broadcast on Saturday afternoons.

(Special thanks to *Mick Plumpton*)

BLUES IN CHICAGO

Chicago blues developed from a mixture of Southern styles brought by black migrant workers from the Mississippi Delta, Arkansas, Louisiana, Alabama and Tennessee to the Illinois metropolis in the late thirties and early forties. By the fifties the powerful sounds of blues bands led by Muddy Waters, Howlin' Wolf and others dominated the national rhythm and blues charts. Their sound of electric guitar, bass, piano, drums and harmonica were to have a profound effect on white rock and roll bands of the sixties — most notably The Rolling Stones.

Chicago remains the foremost blues center in the world and, while few Southern bluesmen have migrated to the city for many years, a new generation of young musicians has grown up on the streets and been influenced by the veterans still working the clubs and bars. There are 30 or more clubs featuring blues, in both traditional and modern styles. Typical Chicago blues taverns offer an intimate, neighborly atmosphere at prices that are hard to beat. Few charge more than a couple of dollars admission and drinks are cheap. Most are located in the black south side of the city, others can be found on the west side, while several clubs in the largely white North Lincoln area book blues on a regular basis.

The magazine *Living Blues* is edited and published out of Chicago by Jim and Amy O'Neal. According to Jim: "Each week the Chicago paper *Reader* lists two or three dozen blues gigs. This information is usually reliable for north side clubs, which advertise regularly, but listings for the black clubs on the south and west sides are sometimes out of date or inaccurate, reflecting the changing nature of the clubs' various policies and the mobility of the musicians. A phone call to verify a listing may help, but there are times when you never know who's playing until after you've paid the door charges and sat down. The pleasant surprises that sometimes result seem to balance the disappointments. There are certain steady gigs that mean good, dependable blues nearly every night of the week and an added attraction is the prospect that just about anybody is likely to show up and do a guest spot. Jamming, or sitting in is encouraged — or at least tolerated — throughout the blues community. New faces, or long-forgotten ones, appear all the time."

"The bad neighborhood syndrome unnecessarily scares many away from clubs in the black areas. It naturally pays to be careful and to find transportation that leaves you close to the club, but it's wrong to construe blues-clubbing as a death-defying mission. There are plenty more dangerous things to do in Chicago than to relax, drink and enjoy music amidst generally friendly, unpretentious people."

Denis Lewis, an English reader of the last edition of this book, told me, "If you don't know your way around this can be a very dangerous city. I think it might be a good idea if you told visitors to take care. With blues clubs it's best if you get someone to show the ropes." One place where you might meet such like-minded blues fans is at the highly respected shop owned by Bob Koester — Delmark Records, 4243 North Lincoln, Chicago, IL 60618, (312) 528-8834.

Steve Tomashefsky of Delmark Records wrote to me after reading this advice and explains, "While we're happy to take as many visitors out to the clubs as we can accommodate, I'd like to stress that the so-called danger of the south and westside clubs is vastly overrated. I suppose it can make the trip more interesting if one imagines one is on safari, but the real charm of most of the clubs is that they are, par excellence, neighborhood taverns, friendly and gemutlich. When someone gets into trouble (and that is very rare), it's usually because he's taking a lot of flash photos or is recording the proceedings on a cassette deck. I should in this context mention that, as far as we're concerned, recording sets in clubs, even as a simple souvenir, without thorough permission from every musician on the stage, cannot be tolerated.

"As for your listings, the advice to check *The Reader* still holds, though it's really a better guide to what happened the previous week than to what will happen during the current. Some people have gotten very upset that a club listed certain musicians in *The Reader*, only to find that they are not there. *The Reader* provides the guide as a service to the clubs, generally, and they are not usually to be construed as official club advertisements.

"The most dependable places are still Theresa's, Checkerboard, Queen Bee, Eddie Shaw's, Ma Bea's and the Majestic M. Actually, almost any printed guide to blues clubs is at least partly out of date as soon as it's printed. The best advice is to call at Delmark Records and ask us for the latest suggestions. We also have a shop downtown at 7 West Grand."

CLUBS IN THE SOUTH OF CHICAGO

Checkerboard Lounge, 423 E. 43rd St., 373-5948. Situated in the worst street in Chicago, this club is a mecca for European blues fans. Owned by Buddy Guy, though he plays here infrequently. Many big-name blues musicians.

Theresa's, 4801 S. Indiana, AT5-2744. Long established tiny basement lounge, on the corner of 48th St. Junior Wells here frequently.

Florence's, 5443 S. Shields, OA4-9658. Sunday afternoon jam sessions. A Chicago version of the rural black Southern juke joint.

Morris Brown's, 4012 S. Indiana, 285-3019.

Queen Bee Lounge, 7401 S. Chicago, 288-9784. Musical fare varies from soul or disco to straight blues. Son Seals, one of the best of the younger generation of Chicago bluesmen, is a favorite here.

Porter's, 5944 S. Halsted, 487-5178.

Cinderella Lounge, 5938 S. Halsted, 488-9290.

Flying Fox, 737 W. 69th. A lonely after-hours club where musicians often come when they've finished a gig. Open until 5AM.

CLUBS IN THE WEST OF CHICAGO

Eddie Shaw's After Hours, 1815 W. Roosevelt, 942-9403. According to Jim O'Neal, "This spacious club is 'Home of the Blues' for singer/saxophonist Shaw and his band The Wolf Gang (former back-up band for Howlin' Wolf). Wolf's specter still looms large in Chicago, and his music lives in the performances of the band and west-side singers like Tail Dagger, Little Wolf Soloman and J.J. Little Wolf Taylor."

Majestic M Lounge, 1422 S. Pulaski, 522-9202. Blues on weekends.

Ma Bea's, 3001 W. Madison, 722-8816.

Riviera, 3200 W. Lake St.

Show and Tell Lounge, 1390 W. Lake, 421-9188.

Tate's Lounge, 1551 S. Kedzie.

David and Thelma's Lounge, 4236 W. Lake, 722-9867.

Palmer's Lounge, 30th and Wentworth. Has had Louis and Dave Myers, Big Moose and Odie Payne with a singer called Willie Buck who's worth hearing.

1125 Club, 1125 W. 59th. Magic Slim's "down to earth blues" here frequently.

CLUBS IN THE NORTH OF CHICAGO

Several clubs feature blues occasionally (check *The Reader* for details). These three nightspots have blues frequently.

Wise Fools Cafe, 2270 N. Lincoln, 929-1510.

Biddy Mulligan's, 7644 N. Sheridan, 761-6532.

Clearwater Saloon, 3447 N. Lincoln, 935-6545.

CHICAGO BLUES ON RECORD

"Today the powerful recording conglomerates show little interest in blues, and most blues singers must depend on small, independent companies which operate from storefronts or producers' homes. The occasional 45s are distributed to ghetto shops, jukeboxes and amateur DJs who shout and spin records in corner taverns. With luck, or enough money, a record might get a little airplay on the radio. The few Chicago companies which issue blues albums deal mainly with a market of white fans, students and collectors. Labels such as Arhoolie, Prestige/Bluesville, Delmark, Testament and Vanguard were instrumental in putting many Chicago bluesmen on LP for the first time in the sixties." (*Jim O'Neal*)

Bruce Iglauer is the head of a small Chicago record label —

Alligator Records — which is recording some of the excellent artists working in the city today. He's issued albums by Son Seals, Fenton Robinson, and Koko Taylor while a recent triple LP set called "Living Chicago Blues" features Pinetop Perkins, Lonnie Brooks Blues Band, The Sons of the Blues, Carey Bell's Blues Harp Band, Magic Slim and the Teardrops, Johnny 'Big Moose' Walker, The Jimmy Johnson Band, Eddie Shaw and the Wolf Gang, and Left Hand Frank and his Blues Band. Write to Bruce at PO Box 60234, Chicago, IL 60660 for a free catalogue. Sonet Records issues Alligator Records throughout Europe.

(Special thanks to *Jim and Amy O'Neal, Steve Tomashefsky* and *Bruce Iglauer*)

COLORADO

Colorado is located in the Rocky Mountains, an area of incredible natural beauty. Most of the musical activity takes place in Denver, the state capital, and Boulder, the student center, while the high class ski resort of Aspen is where you'll find most of the rock stars — relaxing rather than playing — in one of the most beautiful towns in America. Aspen inspired The Eagles to write "The Last Resort" on the album, "Hotel California," the police here drive Saabs, wear denim jackets and don't appear to carry guns!

Colorado has yet to become the major music center it's long promised to be, but there is a growing rock and roll scene and many big name jazz, rock, and country artists perform here frequently. Surprisingly few big names have emerged from this state, rather it has become something of a haven for established names who are tired of life in the Los Angeles fast lane.

There was a time when Colorado seemed set to replace Austin, Texas, as the major country rock center and though the music can still be found in larger doses than anywhere else in the US, there are few new bands taking it up. Lately modern rock and roll has been the source of most of the interesting and innovative new music.

There's a strong local folk and bluegrass scene encouraged by operations like the Biscuit City Record Company who describe themselves as "The voice of the Rockies." Biscuit City has recorded several of the best folk and bluegrass performers in the area, including Dino Arthur, City Limits Bluegrass Band, Dan McCrimmon, Fingers Akimbo and Dan Sadosky. (Biscuit City, 1106 E. 17th Ave., Denver, CO 80218).

Denver

Colorado's "mile-high" city has particularly strong jazz and folk scenes. The folk music tradition goes back to Judy Collins' pioneering days here in the early sixties and has been kept alive by Harry Tufts' Folklore Center. The Colorado Folk Arts Council holds an annual Folklife Festival at the Auditorium Arena in downtown Denver each May. The Denver Jazz club holds an annual Central City Jazz Festival featuring over a dozen Dixieland bands for a long weekend in the middle of August.

Visiting big name rock and jazz acts play major places like the McNichols Arena and Red Rocks. A natural amphitheater in the foothills of the Rocky Mountains not far from Denver, Red Rocks deserves special mention as one of the most attractive open-air arenas anywhere.

Denver is the fourth fastest growing city in the US and the combination of this growth (there are now one million cars in a city of one and a half million people) and the attractive climate of the area is blamed for the fact that it now beats Los Angeles to the unenviable position of the most polluted city in America. Most days Denver is overhung with smog.

CLUBS

Rainbow Music Hall, 6358 E. Evans Ave., 753-1800. This Denver showcase was once a movie house with three halls which were knocked into one 1280-capacity rock club.

Turn of the Century, 7300 E. Hampden Ave., 758-7300. Dinner/buffet and show packages with name performers in rock and soul/disco.

Zeno's, 1421 Larimer St., 623-2104. Dixieland jazz spot.

Clyde's Pub, 4700 Kipling St., 425-1093. Jazz club.

McGaa's, 1761 Market St., 571-4281. Live jazz everynight except Sunday.

Jae Ram Loft, 1431 Ogden St. Local jazz talent.

Bentley's BBC, 1128 Grant St., 861-7877. Coffee house with folk music.

Cafe Nepenthes, 1416 Market St., 534-5423. Varied musical fare nightly from 9PM includes folk, bluegrass and occasional classical groups.

Swallow Hill Music Hall, 604 E. 17th Ave., 832-7280. Folk and jazz spot.

Global Village, 76 S. Pennsylvania St., 778-7214. Long established folk venue.

The Folklore Center, 608 E. 17th Ave., 831-7015. Harry Tufts, a long-time folkie, owns this combined concert hall/rare record shop/repair shop/music school/crafts shop. Local folk talent.

RECORD SHOP

The Malt Shop, 7401 E. Colfax. Doug Krug is the friendly and helpful proprietor of a shop that's an essential stop-off point for fans of progressive country music. Records, books and magazines.

Boulder

Boulder is the university town and quite a magical place that many consider the heart of the Colorado music scene. It's not uncommon for a famous rock personality or two to jam unannounced in Boulder. In the past the town has been privy to some outrageous sneak previews. Clubs in town stay open until 2AM.

Major concerts are held at the Macky Auditorium and the Balch Field House, both on the campus (call 492-6161 for information), and at the Glenn Miller Ballroom named after the famous bandleader who was born here in 1904.

CLUBS

Blue Note Cafe, Pearl Street. Features a range of good music from jazz to rock and country.

Nederlands Pioneer Inn. Noted for booking "the best local talent in a fantastic atmosphere of broken bottles, sweat and spilled beer."

Peggy's Hi Lo Inn, 47th and Diagonal, 442-9211. Country music nightspot.

LOS ANGELES, CALIFORNIA

There's a story that before California was discovered by a Spanish expedition in the 16th century, it was imagined to be a tropical island paradise lost somewhere in the unexplored reaches of the Pacific Ocean and inhabited by strange and fantastic creatures. Imagination has become reality in this "land of the American Dream": Southern California and particularly Los Angeles, "The City of the Angels," where with the right connections and plenty of money, you can enjoy a heaven on earth — a fantastic playground where you can do as you please.

The attraction of Los Angeles, according to Derek Taylor, former publicist of The Beatles and now an executive with WEA Records, is simple: "This town makes no demands on you and it offers you everything good. There seem to be 30 hours in each day and eight days in each week. There is a leisurely pace, but a pace of getting it done. It's all here — the best facilities, the best climate. Everyone you know or like wants to come here!"

Not everyone feels like that about Los Angeles, though. "If you're a member of one of the estimated 3000 acts trying to make it in the music business, it's one of the hardest places on earth, where non-payment for gigs is often the least of your problems: actually getting a gig is often almost impossible. The reason so many youngsters are prepared to put up with impoverished circumstances and awful treatment from some managers and club owners is that the rewards of a record contract can be enormous — and Los Angeles, the capital of the music business, is the best place to chase that contract. Sooner or later every rock act which wants to break into the big time must come and "strut their stuff" in one of the city's clubs. For music fans, the result is an astonishing array of music to be heard every night of the week from musicians trying their hardest to catch the ears of the important record company people who might be lurking in the darker reaches of the clubs.

The late seventies saw an explosion of small nightspots featuring live music. The success of The Knack, a band who moved from playing free gigs in some of Los Angeles' smallest and roughest clubs to headlining 20,000 seat arenas in the space of a few months, has encouraged a renewed interest in the local rock scene which had remained stagnant since the late sixties/early seventies when LA and San Francisco had been producing some of the world's best music.

The Greater Los Angeles area is enormous; it spreads like a patchwork quilt of innumerable communities over 4000 square miles between the mountains and the Pacific Ocean. It's home to over six million people, nearly all of whom seem to know someone in the music business. Los Angeles is crammed with writers, photographers, publicists, managers, limo drivers, clothes designers, messenger services and hundreds of other rock related occupations.

If you've been in San Francisco or New York, with downtowns small enough to walk around, you may find the distances between LA attractions intimidating at first. Even the means of conquering these distances, the super highways, can have a forbidding aspect, especially at a junction like "the stack" where, one above the other, four-, six- and eight-lane freeways carry cars speeding in all directions. However, driving is the easiest way to get around and it really is straight and simple most of the time. If you don't have a license or life in the fast lane looks too terrifying, check out the underrated Southern California Rapid Transit buses that criss-cross the city for a basic fare (ring SCRT for information on 626-4455).

Hollywood is a good place to choose as a base for operations. The major clubs are fairly accessible from there — a late taxi back to your hotel isn't going to bankrupt you — and so is the infamous Sunset Strip, where the billboards, considered by many as a unique art form, extol the virtues of the latest offering from countless rock personnel. While you are on the Strip try to locate the building where Ed Byrnes stood outside combing his hair every week in the "77 Sunset Strip" TV series. Give you a clue though — it isn't 77. Incidentally, if your taste in music leans towards the bizarre, the most outrageous sounds you're likely to hear in Los Angeles don't come from The Whisky or the Roxy, but from a small suburb called Anaheim, Disneyland no less, where the Country Bear Jamboree is definitely worth checking out should you find yourself in the "Magic Kingdom." Imagine, if you can, the Muppets playing the Grand Ole Opry and you begin to get the picture.

Big name rock, country and soul acts play at the enormous Anaheim Stadium, The Forum in Inglewood, The Hollywood Bowl, The Universal Amphitheatre, The Santa Monica Civic Auditorium and the Greek Theater. These are not always the best places to see and hear your favorite musicians, but the phenomenal demand for rock concert tickets in this area is such that playing in smaller, more suitable places is often out of the question. The Rolling Stones and Bruce Springsteen had frustrating times trying to organize small club dates in addition to their impersonal big stadium concerts. Springsteen played a surprise gig at The Roxy which, though arguably the best concert the famous club has ever presented, resulted in tremendous acrimony and bitterness from the thousands denied tickets.

A number of rhythm and blues performers including Roy Brown, Roy Milton, Charles Brown, Percy Mayfield and Paul Gayden, best known for their recordings in the forties and fifties, are still appearing in nightspots in and around Los Angeles, though it requires a bit of detective work to track them down. Buy a copy of the weekly black newspaper *LA Sentinel*, published each Thursday, and check the club listings. The Diamond Head, Tiki's Lounge on South West Avenue and the Parisian Room at La Brea and Washington feature blues artists from time to time. Joe Liggins, the city blues musician who recorded for Specialty in the late forties and early fifties, plays piano with the assistance of a drum machine at Bogart's, a restaurant/disco at Long Beach.

Two free weekly papers provide a comprehensive guide to the live music scene: *LA Weekly* and *Reader*. There's also the free bimonthly *BAM* which has good features on up-and-coming California bands, and the *Los Angeles Times Calendar*, which appears every Sunday, lists live music events.

CLUBS

The Roxy, 9009 Sunset Blvd., West Hollywood, 878-2222 (for credit card reservations call charge line 520-8010). Once the Largo Strip House, though all that remains of those days is the fancy vaudeville curtain. The Roxy Theater is now the most prestigious showcase club in the capital of the music business. Capacity 600, waitress service — everyone sits at tables, there's no room for dancing — this is an excellent place to see and hear good music. Shows are at 9:30 and 11PM. Reservations are often advisable as tickets can be scarce, especially when a record company decides to "paper the house" — buying up most of the tickets when they are showcasing a new act. Engagements vary from anything from one to five nights — a typical week could feature such a varied bill as bluesman Bobby Bland, country star Emmylou Harris and the Hot Band, contemporary rockers The Cars and soul songstress Betty Wright. British writer Chris Welch wrote about The Roxy in *Melody Maker*: "It's a shame there's nothing like it in London. In LA at least, rock fans are treated like adults and the result is an amazingly hip and friendly atmosphere." Next door to The Roxy is the famous Rainbow Bar and Grill where you can eat, drink and do a bit of star spotting at the same time. Also very close by is The Whisky A Go Go and Tower Records.

Whisky A Go Go, 8901 Sunset Blvd., West Hollywood, 652-4202. In the mid-sixties this was the trendy Los Angeles nightspot — a sparkling club where girls used to dance in cages suspended from the ceiling. After a period in decline the club is now an important West Hollywood place, again thanks to an imaginative booking policy that brings in the best of new wave rock — Elvis Costello made his LA debut here. Soul/disco acts and rock 'n' roll artists from the fifties, like Carl Perkins, are making comebacks. Two shows a night at 9 and 11PM.

Doug Weston's Troubadour, 9081 Santa Monica Blvd., West Hollywood, 276-6168. The original Troubadour was a jazz club on La Cienega, but in the early sixties it relocated to Santa Monica Blvd. in West Hollywood as a folk club. In 1967 owner Doug Weston started booking rock bands, though the Monday Hoot Night was retained from the folkie days and is still going today. The club became the launching pad to fame for innumerable stars of the future — Joni Mitchell and Elton John are two that immediately spring to mind — and the bar became an infamous hangout for musicians and groupies. The club experienced hard times when the Roxy opened and many feared it would have to close, but the late seventies' boom in local rock bands brought the crowds back and it's a very popular spot once again. The Knack sprang to fame from here after their nineteen date series of gigs here in 1978 — the little known bands playing here today could be tomorrow's rock heroes.

Madame Wong's Restaurant, 949 Sun Mun Way at the Broadway Gate in Chinatown, 624-5346. The new wave rock explosion produced unusual new nightspots as well as bands. This was an ornate Chinese restaurant where exotic Hawaiian dancers used to perform under a thatched roof — now new wave rock acts play two sets a night, at 9:30 and 11PM, amidst the same Oriental decor.

Hong Kong Cafe, 425 Gin Ling Way, Chinatown, 858-6907. The success of Madame Wong's inspired this elaborately decorated Chinese restaurant to start booking local rock acts to perform among the gilt dragons.

Club 88, 11784 Pico Blvd., West Los Angeles, 479-6923. Young Los Angeles musicians regard most club owners with deep distrust and suspicion, yet they all love Wayne Maynotte, a former World War II pilot and the unlikely owner of this rock club. Gigs here pay good money — often as much as $400. According to the *LA Weekly*, "He's perhaps the only club owner willing to risk booking unknown bands, which are usually spurned because they lack a proven following. Many of the rock circuit's current idols have him to thank for rescuing them from limbo." Music nightly from 9:30.

The Starwood, 8151 Santa Monica Blvd., West Hollywood, 656-2200. Another of the most popular and innovative Hollywood rock clubs, this was once P.J.'s, a black club, and is situated in the seedy porn-book area of Santa Monica Blvd. Imaginative booking policy draws many musicians among the spectators which is always an important indication of a good nightspot. Local rock, name blues and R&B talent.

Gazzarri's, 9039 Sunset Blvd., West Hollywood, 273-6606. This must be the oldest rock club in Los Angeles having recently passed its twentieth year. The launching pad to fame for bands that include The Doors and Van Halen, it features the best local rock bands.

McCabe's Guitar Shop, 3101 Pico Blvd., Santa Monica, 828-4497. McCabe's is a delightful shop combined with a 100-seat listening room. One of the few places in the area where you can hear good acoustic music. Occasional name acts like Mike Bloomfield, Tom Paxton and Merle Travis while Jackson Browne, Tom Waits and Linda Ronstadt have played special benefit shows here in the last few years. A place where unexpected musical surprises can, and frequently do, happen. Highly recommended.

Palomino, 6907 Lankershim Blvd., 765-9256. For anyone with a taste for country music, this great club in North Hollywood has to be the first place to visit in Los Angeles. For over 20 years The Palomino has showcased almost every country artist of note, though it no longer has a clearly defined "country only" policy and jazz, rockabilly and R&B acts appear occasionally. In the late sixties the Flying Burrito Brothers were the house band and years earlier people like Glen Campbell were regulars. Shows are twice nightly at 8 and 11PM and there's a talent night once a week. The food's been recommended by several visitors. The world famous Nudies Rodeo Tailors is nearby (see below) and worth visiting if you're in the area.

The Lighthouse, 30 Pier Ave., Hermosa Beach, 372-6911. Jazz fans returning to Los Angeles after an absence of many years will find this club hasn't changed much at all; it's still small with an intimate atmosphere and featuring fine jazz from some well known and respected musicians. Surveying the rest of the Los Angeles jazz scene they'll be pleasantly surprised, astonished even, at the increase in nightspots featuring jazz. There are dozens of jazz clubs, too many to mention here, so check the *LA Weekly* for details. Visitors will need a car, because many of the best places are some way from the center of Los Angeles — and money, because several clubs are small and have to charge a lot to cover their overheads.

Donte's, 4769 Lankershim Blvd., 877-8347. An intimate, popular jazz venue in North Hollywood near the homes of such stars as Bob Hope and Ricky Nelson. A dinner club — the food is excellent — it seats less than 100 people, is expensive but a great place to hear bebop orientated jazz. A musician's hangout, so impromptu jam sessions are always a possibility.

Concerts By The Sea, 100 Fisherman's Wharf, Redondo Beach, 379-4998. Probably Los Angeles' top jazz club in terms of the major acts it manages to book — Woody Herman, Horace Silver, Gary Burton, Jon Hendricks. Music from 9PM Thursdays to Sundays. A concert hall — you sit in rows — with excellent sight lines and sound.

The clubs listed above are among the most popular and best known places in Los Angeles. Below are listed the best of the rest, again grouped into rock, country/folk and jazz.

The Rock Corporation, 14310 Oxnard St., Van Nuys, 989-0661. Popular, crowded, hot and sweaty. Jeff Simon owns this small club that features occasional name bands but unusually local boogie outfits.

Bla Bla Cafe, 12446 Ventura Blvd., Studio City, 769-7874. Best known for folkies and comedy acts, now booking modern rock outfits. Music from 11PM.

Blackie's, 607 N. La Brea, Hollywood, 932-8408. The jukebox here provides you with an excellent opportunity to check out the best local talent — several of the selections are small label singles featuring Los Angeles' finest. It's also a good place for live music: local rock and pop bands.

Blue Lagune Saloon, 4080 Lincoln Blvd., Marina del Ray, 822-9121. Atmospheric local rock club.

The Londoner, 1530 Lincoln Blvd., Santa Monica, 395-4336. Rock club that's supposed to resemble a British pub though English visitors usually turn their noses up at the imported beer — a British brew that's one of the least liked, or drunk, by rock fans at home!

Pan-Andreas Theater, 8325 Santa Monica Blvd., 654-8780. Small theater with an enormous stage means that local rock bands can imagine what it'll be like when they make the big time. No alcohol.

The Banjo Cafe, 2906 Lincoln Blvd., Santa Monica, 392-5716. Bluegrass with a relaxed, pleasant atmosphere. Good sound from bands, usually talented local aggregrations. Music nightly plus Sunday lunchtime jam sessions.

Cal's Corral, 16714 Hawthorne, Lawndale, 371-2257. Texas-style country music club that features talented local bands like Stone Creek who mix progressive country with classics from the past. $1 admission.

The Foothill Club, 1922 Cherry Ave., Signal Hill, Long Beach. Long-established traditional country club with a large dance floor.

The Palace Saloon, 21211 Sherman Way, Canoga Park, 346-8966. Open Thursdays to Sundays for country rock sounds from local bands like Southbound or Prairie Siren.

Topanga Corral, 2034 N. Topanga Canyon Blvd., Topanga, 455-1310. Good local bands in a Texan honky-tonk atmosphere.

The Baked Potato, 3787 Cahuenga Blvd. West, 980-1615. Small restaurant and jazz club.

Carmelo's, 4449 Van Nuys Blvd., Sherman Oaks, 995-9532. Variety of talented down-to-earth jazz trios.

Comeback Inn, 1633 W. Washington Blvd., Venice, 396-7255. Small, popular jazz spot. No cover.

Jazzpot, 3344 E. Coast Hwy., Corona Del Mar (714) 673-7181. Jazz seven nights a week.

Pasquale's, 22724 Pacific Coast Hwy., Malibu, 456-2007. Owned by bassist Pat Senatore who plays here frequently with his own trio, Pasquale's has views of the Pacific through the glass walls. A wonderful location to hear good jazz.

Parisian Room, La Brea and Washington, 936-8704. Quality jazz and blues singers.

Soundroom, 11616 Ventura Blvd., Studio City, 761-3555. Imaginative booking policy with variety of local jazz acts from duos to big bands.

RECORD SHOPS

There are over two pages of listings of record shops in the Los Angeles yellow pages and collectors would be advised to check through them. I've listed only a selection of the good shops below — all have been recommended.

Tower Records, 8801 Sunset Strip, 657-7300. Close to the Roxy and the Whisky is the main branch of a chain of stores that tries to stock every record in print. No other chain on the West Coast carries such a varied stock. Visitors from small towns will find the sight of so many records together in one place quite breathtaking. The best blues section (apart from Muskadine Music in Santa Monica) to be found anywhere and the gospel section is quite unbelievable. Thousands of deletions and lots of free magazines. Other branches of Tower Records, "open every nite of the year 'til midnight," in this area: 1028 Westwood Boulevard, Westwood Village; 9717 Van Nuys (corner of Van Nuys and Parthenia), Panorama City; 306 N. Beach Blvd., between Lincoln and Knott's Berry Farm, Anaheim.

Muskadine Music, 212 Pier Ave., Santa Monica, 392-1136. Highly respected shop managed by Mary Aldin and connected with Down Home Music (see San Francisco). A classy selection of jazz, blues, R&B, old timey and bluegrass. Magazines, fanzines and tuition books. Nice, friendly staff.

McCabe's Guitar Shop, 3101 Pico Blvd., Santa Monica, 828-8037. This combined book, record and musical instrument shop has already been listed under clubs because of its listening room. Interesting selection of folk records. The helpful staff will direct you to other good stores in this area.

Record Depot Inc., 1604 N. Highland, 464-9926. Dealing in new and second-hand records, this shop has some astonishing bargains. Records from 15¢. One writer claims, "I've picked up sealed albums for little over a dollar that have only been released a week or two!" Stocks move fast — a must if you're in the area. Very good for cut-price disco records.

Rhino Records, one store on Pico Blvd., 473-1518, another on W. Westwood, 474-8685. Claim to have the largest selection of deletions in town. According to Ray Coleman, "This place is amazing! The first thing you see on entering is a display announcing, 'We regretfully announce that the fascist pig record companies have raised the price of our new releases; we urge you to show your disgust by not buying these records.' It doesn't stop there, elsewhere in the store are other manifestations of independence; a cardboard cut-out of John Denver with a noose round his neck."

Discontinued Records, 444 S. Victory Blvd., 849-4791. Stacks of rarities and hard to find stuff. No bargains though — the staff are very knowledgeable about their stock and some albums are quite expensive.

HONKY TONKIN'

Cosmopolitan Book Shop, 7007 Melrose, 938-7119. One block east of La Brea is a book store with a large and interesting selection of second-hand albums at good prices.

Jazzland Records, Santa Monica and Inglewood (check phone book for details). An operation that's aimed at jazz record collectors. They sell mainly cut-out product. Mail order address P.O. Box 984, Topanga, California 90290.

Poo Bah, 1101 Easy Walnut St., Pasadena. A very large selection of promo discs and used records. Prices vary according to condition but you can buy second-hand records from 30¢.

Moby Disc, S. Victory Blvd., San Fernando Valley. "Best record store around with at least 15 racks of cheap records."

RECORD LABEL

Rollin' Rock Records, 6918 Peach Ave., Van Nuys, California 91406. Rockabilly was a phenomenon of the fifties, regarded by many collectors as the purest form of rock 'n' roll. One of the most revered rockabilly singers, Charlie Feathers, believes the music is a combination of bluegrass and cottonpatch blues (rhythmic, intense Mississippi country blues) — the bluegrass provided the fast pace and the blues provided the feel and the slapped rhythm. Rollin' Rock is a remarkable little rockabilly record company run by Ron Weisner who immigrated to LA from Europe in the sixties. Ron, who is first and foremost a fan, began by leasing old masters of his favorite rockabilly recordings and then progressed to finding singers from the fifties, and then youngsters with a feel for the music, and recording them in a primitive studio in the front room of his house. Some of these early re-creations weren't very good, but more recently he's produced records that sound both fresh and authentic. Rollin' Rock artists like Ray Campi and The Rebels appear locally and are well worth seeing. Write to Ron for an up-to-date catalogue.

SPECIALIST SHOP

Nudie's Rodeo Tailors Inc., 5015 Lankershim Blvd., North

Hollywood, 762-3105 and 877-9505. A large and impressive store that's well worth a visit even if you don't intend to buy anything. Nudie is internationally known as a designer of clothes for country musicians, TV personalities and film stars. There are numerous signed photographs (including one of a very young Rick Nelson) and personalized belt buckles that have been presented to Nudie by grateful customers.

RADIO

According to respected LA writer Harvey Kubernik, "Los Angeles is a city of freedom: probably one of the few in the world to offer 20 different kinds of rock music on the AM and FM dial." Check the daily papers for the wavelength details of Los Angeles' many radio stations whose formats range from disco, A.O.R. (adult oriented radio), oldies, beautiful music (probably the most popular radio format in Southern California — it oozes out of most public buildings and elevators), country, Spanish, top 40 rock, mellow rock, talk and soul. KMET 94.7 FM, KLOS 95.5 FM, and KWST 105.9 FM are the most popular rock stations; KLAC 570 AM and KGBS 97.1 FM are good country stations; KDAY 1580 AM and KUTE 101.9 FM are soul and disco stations; KMPC 710 AM is a personality station where you can find Gary Owens, the announcer from the old "Laugh In" TV show, and Wink Martindale, who had a big hit with "Deck of Cards" years ago; KRLA 1110 AM plays mostly oldies; and KKGO 105.1 is a jazz station. Los Angeles rock character Rodney Bingheimer has a late night show on KROQ 106.7 FM.

(Special thanks to *Barry Ballard* and *Terry Andrews*).

MEMPHIS, TENNESSEE

Several musical travelers have gone to Memphis expectantly humming "Beale Street Blues" or "Memphis, Tennessee" to themselves, only to find nothing but a statue of W.C. Handy and Elvis Presley's mansion. Peter Sherster, owner of Red Lightnin' Records, was one such disappointed visitor — "I couldn't find any live music there at all, except in the Square on Sunday afternoon when the reverend would swing with a dynamic bass, guitar and drums gospel group and shout to the guitarist 'Turn that axe *down* boy'."

Memphis, though steeped in blues and rock 'n' roll history, is surprisingly lacking in an active live music scene. The last time I was there the police were on strike and an 8PM curfew effectively closed any clubs I might have found. However Memphis residents and a few fortunate visitors tell me this city can be musically rewarding though it takes a fair bit of effort and good luck.

For much of this century Memphis has been an important and influential music city. It was here in the early 1900s that W.C. Handy, the "Father of the Blues," composed a campaign song for Mayor E. G. Crump called "Memphis Blues" and then "St. Louis Blues," both of which became nationally famous. They were written in the Beale Street area which was one of the most dangerous and violent places in America at the time and earned the city the tag "murder capital of the US." The blues migrated here from the farms of west Tennessee and the Mississippi Delta — Memphis always having been a key stopping point for those enroute to the Northern cities in search of work — and early field recordings were made in the Beale Street area in the twenties and thirties. In addition to blues, the clubs and bars of the street resounded to the sounds of jazz and hillbilly music, though this went largely unrecorded.

None of the nightspots of the old Beale Street have been preserved though the area is involved in a great urban renewal program and a kind of "Preservation Hall" is planned that is supposedly going to utilize "the unique architecture of the period." The Beale Street Blue Light entertainment area was scheduled to have at least two clubs where blues would be featured. W.C. Handy's statue is in a park close to Beale Street and a combined store and museum — Schwab's Store, 163 Beale Street — has been recommended. As British blues enthusiast Ken Smith explains, "If you're a blues freak and you find yourself on Beale Street go to this store and take a look at their museum. Mr. Schwab (a true gent) himself will show you around. Don't worry, you won't have to ask him — he'll probably introduce himself before you get past the voodoo counter just inside the front door. His stories of Beale Street in the twenties are fascinating. Worth a visit."

Much of the wealth of Memphis music went unrecorded until the opening of the first recording studio in 1950. Memphis Recording Service was set up by a former radio announcer called Sam Phillips. After two years of leasing recordings to record companies he set up his own, Sun Records, in 1952. The list of important artists that Phillips recorded at 706 Union Avenue is staggering and includes rhythm and blues performers Junior Parker and Rufus Thomas, rock 'n' rollers Elvis Presley, Roy Orbison, Jerry Lee Lewis, Carl Perkins and two men, best known these days as country singers, Charlie Rich and Johnny Cash.

The success of Sun stimulated other people in Memphis to start record companies including Hi where the Bill Black Combo recorded a string of hits in the sixties and where soul singers Al Green and the underrated Ann Peebles are still recording today. Sun ceased to be an important and influential label in the sixties and its place as the main Memphis record company was taken by Stax which had been formed by a white named Jim Stewart, a former bank teller and country music fiddle player. At his studios on McLemore

Street, the distinctive soul sound of Stax was created that led to numerous hits for acts like Johnnie Taylor, Booker T and the MGs, Sam and Dave, Eddie Floyd and the incomparable Otis Redding who recorded for the Stax subsidiary Volt. The company fell to pieces in the mid-seventies through financial mis-management but is today trying to re-establish itself with the sponsorship of the West Coast company Fantasy.

Elvis Presley was born in Tupelo, Mississippi, but moved to Memphis with his parents when he was eight. His earliest — and many would agree his best — recordings were made in Memphis with Sam Phillips. He lived and died at his mansion Graceland, 3764 Elvis Presley Blvd., Whitehaven, South Memphis. You can't get into the house but can walk through the 14-acre grounds and see his gravestone in the Meditation Garden.

In sharp contrast to the magnificence of Graceland is the two-room shack where Elvis was born in the poorest part of Tupelo on 8 January 1933. Jane and Michael Stern visited Tupelo (which is about 100 miles from Memphis) for their book *Amazing America* (Random House) and found that a Mrs. Billie Boyd had turned the dilapidated shack into a national shrine. It can be visited in the afternoon or by appointment — phone 842-6640. The Sterns explain, "She has made everything as authentic as possible — although the area is no longer a soulful swamp, and the house does look a bit cleaner than it might have looked when Saltillo Road was only a muddy path running through the woods." (Elvis Presley Park, Saltillo Road, Tupelo, Mississippi.)

A favorite cult figure for rockabilly fans is Charlie Feathers who still lives in Memphis. He collaborated with Elvis on his early pioneering recordings for Sun and co-wrote "I Forgot to Remember to Forget." He never had anything approaching a hit record, but his fifties recordings are now regarded as classics and original copies change hands for small fortunes. He remains true to rockabilly today and still plays with a band that includes his son Bubba. A reader of the last edition of the guide saw him at Mr. T's, a club at the junction of Sumner and White Station and thought he was a regular performer there.

Big name rock and soul acts occasionally play Memphis at the Mid-South Coliseum, the Liberty Bowl Memorial Center, the Cook Convention Center Auditorium and the 50-year-old Orpheum Theater on Main Street. The area around Overton Square is supposed to be good for clubs, bars and restaurants; it's located a few minutes' drive east of downtown on Madison at Cooper Street.

The Friday morning edition of the Memphis daily paper provides the best guide for gigs while the monthly magazine *The City of Memphis* is sometimes helpful for locating interesting music.

CLUBS

Savarin's Blues Alley, 60 South Front. Downtown by the river. "Good for blues — Big Sam plays here, he's a Smiley Lewis imitator and plays good piano."

The Mall. Once a club called The Ritz, this is one of the best places for local rock.

V.F.W. in the north Memphis suburb of Frayser. Mostly rockabilly and country. Marcus Van Story here at weekends.

RECORD BUYING

Selecto Records, Chelsea Avenue. Selecto took a good part of the old Sun stock after it was sold. The problem is that people are untidy and vicious. Paul Slattery reports that he found mint Warren Smith 78s here that had been deliberately mutilated with a key — presumably so that the person's own mint copies would become rarer and even more valuable.

Collector's Recordland, Box 16786, Memphis, Tennessee 38116, (901) 396-6745. Jim Stapleton runs this rock 'n' roll records mail order service. He's proved very helpful to foreign readers of this guide in the past and serious collectors might be advised to contact him before they visit the city.

NASHVILLE, TENNESSEE

"Music City USA" has probably more talented musicians per square inch than anywhere else in America, but they rarely perform publicly in their home town. As John Lomax who knows the city well observes, "Don't come to Nashville if you crave live music every night. Despite a plethora of pickers the city lacks a vital club scene. Most of the music is confined to the studios because the artists who come to Nashville come either to record or to rest from the rigors of the road."

Dedicated country music fans will love the place because there's so much for them to see and do — guided tours past the homes of the stars with their guitar shaped swimming pools, museums and exhibitions, record and souvenir shops, and historic buildings. The next chapter will guide you to the country music points of interest.

Nashville is known as "The Athens of the South" due to the large number of educational esablishments and an abundance of historical and cultural landmarks, including a full-sized replica of the Parthenon used to great effect in the finale of the film "Nashville." The city has 700 churches and is sometimes known as "The Buckle of the Bible Belt." Go out into the Tennessee backwaters and you could find yourself stumbling upon one of the outlawed "Holy Roller" sects holding a secret tent ceremony where members dance with poisonous snakes round their necks or drink dangerous mixtures of strychnine and water as "acts of faith."

Nashville isn't the easiest of places for the visiting music fan, especially traveling alone and without his own means of transport. Hotels are expensive unless you're prepared to risk one of the dingy, often dangerous, places near the bus station, and the public transport system is poor compared to most American cities. Finding out what's on isn't easy as there's no weekly paper with reliable gig listings and the clubs don't seem in the habit of advertising in the daily paper *The Tennessean.* Telephone the clubs to find out who's playing or ask people in the Goldrush Bar (opposite The Exit/In) during the early evening "Happy Hour."

Most of the best music in Nashville happens in studios or at private functions. If you make friends with some of the pickers you could try to get in on the private party circuit, but that takes time. The bars near the Exit/In are probably the best places to make such friends.

CLUBS

Exit/In, 2208 Elliston Place, 327-2784. Showcase club dedicated to presenting all types of good music. Weekday shows 8 and 10:30PM, weekends 8 and 11PM. The club was opened about 10 years ago and has had three extensions built, but it's still often too small to cater to everybody who wants to get in. Capacity 300. Cover varies from $5 to over $10. Twice a month there are "Writers' Nights" that showcase up-and-coming talent in a series of 20-minute sets. There are occasional "Performers Nights" with better known acts than on the writers' evenings and about four performers doing 40-minute sets.

Studio One, 2206 Elliston Place. Next door to the Exit/In. Local rock and white soul/funk bands featured.

Picking Parlor, Downtown at 105 2nd Ave., 256-5720. A small club that often features interesting acts. "Really jumps at weekends."

Mississippi Whiskers, 1713 Church St., 320-9118. Occasional name acts, local talent and frequent "Writer's Nights." A good place to see local favorites like the talented jazz guitarist Lenny Breau.

Wind In The Willows, 2205 State St., 320-9154. Music every night from 8:30 at this club situated not far from Elliston Place. Hubert Davis and the Season Travelers play bluegrass from Wednesday to Sunday.

Bluegrass Inn, at the rear of 1914 Broadway, the **The Dusty Road Tavern**, across the river from the center of town at 114 Woodland Street, are also recommended. Full details at the end of the next chapter.

RADIO

WSM is Nashville's best known radio station. It was started in 1925 by an insurance company which quickly hit on the successful idea of using country music to sell insurance to working class whites. WSM (standing for "We Shield Millions") broadcasts on 650 AM and is one of several country stations. Others include WKDA 1240 AM (contemporary country), WENO 1430 AM and WSIX 97.9 FM. WVOL 1470 AM plays soul while 91.1 FM and WKDF 103.3 FM program rock.

(Special thanks to *John Lomax* and *Alan Messer*).

stax

THE NIGHTHAWKS

EXIT/IN
Nashville's Music Forum

COUNTRY FAN'S GUIDE TO MUSIC CITY, USA

Nashville, Tennessee, is the country music capital of the world, site of dozens of recording studios and record company offices, and hundreds of publishing houses. Each year it is a mecca for tens of thousands of country fans eager to visit the source of their favorite music.

It's surprising to discover that 98% of the people and places in "Music City USA" have nothing whatever to do with country music. The big business here is money, insurance being the largest part of it, a multi-billion dollar operation compared to the multi-millions the music industry generates. The people in the music business work in a small area that is easily avoided, ignored even, by the rest of the town. Most of the things the country fan will be interested in are in the business area, Music Row; the downtown Broadway area where the Nashville music industry used to be based; and Opryland, the family-style entertainment center that contains the new Grand Ole Opry Building.

The one time heart of country music, Broadway, downtown near the Greyhound station, is depressing these days. The area has become extremely run down and, side by side with souvenir shops and tourist attractions, there are strip clubs and adult book stores. Attempts have been made to clean up the area but without success. The biggest attraction here is The Ryman Auditorium on 116 Fifth Avenue North. This home of the Grand Ole Opry for over 30 years is open to the public every day from 8:30AM to 4:30PM.

Thomas Ryman was a riverboat captain, notorious for his drinking and gambling. One day, so the story goes, he went to an evangelical meeting with the intention of breaking it up but underwent an astonishing conversion as a result of the Rev. Sam Jones' sermon on motherhood and paid for the building of an auditorium that the good reverend could use for his work. The building was used exclusively for religious purposes for about six years, then went over to classical music concerts until 1941 when it became the home of the Opry.

Performers and country music lovers have fond memories of the old building but weren't sorry to leave the cramped changing rooms, the hard wooden pews (a reminder of the building's original purpose) and the lack of air conditioning, for the new Opry.

Just around the corner from the Ryman is Tootsie's Orchid Lounge at 422 Broadway. For years unknown pickers, fresh off the Greyhound bus, would come to this little beer joint in the hope of being discovered by one of the country music stars who patronized the bar between performances at the Opry. Tootsie's customers these days are tourists who come to stare at the memento-lined walls and to listen to the house band "The Orchid Loungers." The famous owner Hattie Louise "Tootsie" Bess died in 1978 after a long battle against cancer. She was known for her habit of ejecting rowdy customers with the aid of a long hat pin. Among the wreaths at her funeral was a heart made of flowers with a large hat pin stuck through the center, sent by Ernest Tubb.

The Alamo is the most famous clothes shop in the Broadway area. Famous country names have been coming here for years to buy their stage costumes. Nearby is one of the chain of Loretta Lynn Western Stores where you can buy everything from cowboy boots to horse saddles.

Ernest Tubb's famous record shop is at 417 Broadway. For many years it was the home of the "Midnight Jamboree" radio program, broadcast live every Friday night over WSM.

About a mile from the Broadway area are 16th and 17th Avenues which, with their inter-connecting streets, make up the section of Nashville known as Music Row. This is the heart of the music industry today where you'll find most of the studios and offices. This is where the record executives do their wheeling and dealing, and where the hits are made. Poor songwriters in search of publishers and music journalists in search of free records like the layout of Music Row because everything is close together and therefore within walking distance. This area overflows with talent and for the sharp-eyed there's usually a famous name or two to be glimpsed through windows or jumping into cars.

The best place for country fans to go is the junction of 16th Avenue, Division and Demonbreun Street, where there are a number of places of interest and the starting points of bus trips that take you past the homes of the stars, to local beauty spots and sometimes on tours that take you inside studios, etc.

Best of all is The Country Music Hall of Fame and Museum at 4 Music Square East. Run by the Country Music Foundation, which was formed with the specific aim of creating a museum and library devoted to country music, it opened in 1967 but was extensively remodeled and expanded in 1977. It incorporates several exhibits, displays being periodically changed and modified, and at least one completely new exhibit is created each year.

Among the many exhibits you'll find are "The History of Country Music," a slide show; Thomas Hart Benton's mural "The Source of Country Music," a movie theater showing short films of historic country music makers; Elvis Presley's "Solid Gold Cadillac"; instrument and memorabilia displays; "A Song Is Born," an eight-minute presentation of a Music City style recording session that demonstrates how the "Nashville Sound" is created; "The Country Music Hall of Fame" featuring plaques and portraits honoring the careers of those elected individuals, artists and nonperformers who've made a major contribution towards the development of country music; and a country store with souvenirs.

Across the road from the museum you'll find a replica of Webb Pierce's guitar-shaped swimming pool. For $2 you can see the pool (though sadly you aren't allowed a quick dip), Webb's $100,00 car and get a "free" hit record.

The music being produced in Nashville's studios these days is increasingly diverse, and the up-and-coming young record company executives have taken the word "country" off their cards — they now talk about making "Nashville music" and are fond of saying, "There are two types of music — good and bad." Down among the tourist spots at the end of Music Row this wind of change has had no effect — everything is very much traditional country. At 117 16th Avenue you'll find a large souvenir shop called Country Corner where you can buy Dolly Parton dolls (with moving parts), Goo Goo Candy bars (named after the initials of the Grand Ole Opry and advertised there for years), bumper stickers saying "Keep It Country," postcards, etc. Some of the souvenirs here are crude, others remarkably tasteless. How about a set of bullet hole decals, "terrific on car windows — looks like you've been shot at!"

The Conway Twitty Record Shop is at 1530 Deomonbreun Street. It's well stocked with records and souvenirs. The price of albums and singles here isn't cheap, but it does have the advantage of carrying a lot of back catalogue items. For the foreign visitor this is a goldmine because there are hundreds of albums that have never been released outside the US.

Still in the Music Row area there is Feature Sound Studio, 1302 Division Street, where you can attend a live demonstration of a recording session. Daily 9 to 5, admission $2. The Country Wax

Museum at 118 16th Avenue South has 50 "life-like figures of famous country music entertainers."

Down at 1300 Division Street is the War Memorial Auditorium, home of the Nashville Jubilee which was established in 1977 and is seen by some people as the cutting edge of the movement to rid country music of the rock and pop influences. The Jubilee holds performances on weekend nights featuring two or three big names and draws largely from the overflow of tourists who can't get seats for the oversubscribed Opry. The atmosphere is not unlike the old Ryman days with fans encouraged to come down front to speak to entertainers and get autographs. Between acts there are pre-recorded tapes urging people to call their local DJs when they get home and tell them to "keep it country." Shows are at 8PM and you can book (256-5125), but there are almost always seats available.

Nine miles out of town, just off Interstate 40, is Opryland, a gigantic amusement park with a musical theme. There are shows reflecting all kinds of American music, there's Hill Country with folk and bluegrass, and a 50s area with a rock 'n' roll section. The Opry Plaza is the main focal point with the new Opry House and the Roy Acuff museum.

The park has a number of spectacular rides that have musical names like The Wabash Cannonball, a terrifying rollercoaster that takes you screaming through 360° loops at speeds that seem to be over 100 mph. Much calmer is the "Tennessee Waltz," a sedate carousel. Opryland also has a park with buffalo, elk and longhorn steers.

The Grand Ole Opry is now housed at 2800 Opryland Drive, a purpose-built theater seating 4400. The radio show, which has run every Saturday night on WHN for 53 years without missing a broadcast, has grown from humble beginnings to big business.

For most us the name Grand Ole Opry is synonymous with country. It all began with George D. Hay, the self styled "Solemn Old Judge," standing in front of a microphone at WSM studios in Nashville and introducing an 80-year-old fiddler called Uncle Jimmy Thompson who claimed to be able to "fiddle the bugs off a 'tater vine'." After a fitful start WSM Barn Dance began regular broadcasting in December 1925 but changed its name soon after Hay's ad-libbed retort to a pompous announcer from the previous program, "You've been up in the clouds with Grand Opera, now get down to earth in a 4-hour shindig of Grand Ole Opry."

The program moved from the radio station to a number of temporary homes including the Hillsboro Theater, the Dixie Tabernacle and the War Memorial Building. Early favorites included Dr. Humphrey Bate and his daughter Alcyone, the Crook Brothers and Kirk McGee and the ever popular Uncle Dave Macon. In the twenties and thirties instrumental music, mainly banjo and fiddle, dominated and any singing was incidental. All this changed in 1938 with the arrival of the Opry's very first singing star, Roy Acuff. With songs like 'Wabash Cannonball' and 'The Great Speckled Bird,' he quickly became very popular and paved the way for more singing stars like Ernest Tubb and Eddy Arnold.

After being presented from a number of different buildings the Opry finally found a permanent home at the Ryman Auditorium in 1941. The next fifteen years saw the show grow side-by-side with the country music business. The Opry can take much of the credit for establishing Nashville as the country music capital and launching many of the major country stars like Marty Robbins, Hank Williams and Lefty Frizzell.

The arrival of rock 'n' roll in the mid-fifties delivered a death blow to many of the radio barn dances and the Opry only survived with difficulty. The Nashville-based record companies found they had to change their music radically in the early sixties to compete with the rock boom but the Opry retained the traditional approach—something hard-core country fans will always be grateful for. Today the Opry is no longer so important to the music business with many of the big names either shunning it or finding they can't commit themselves to the number of nights a year required as a member.

Nevertheless the Opry today is more popular than ever, and visitors have to book their tickets months in advance to be sure of a seat. The move from the Ryman came in 1974 and the new hall has modern air conditioning and comfortable seats in contrast to the old buildings' wooden church pews. The stars still mill around the stage area during the performances, *and* you are allowed to take photographs.

More than 60 artists are members of the Opry today and you'll see 15 or more at an evening show, eight or more at a matinee. Stars include Roy Acuff, Hank Snow, comedienne Minnie Pearl and modern names like Larry Gatlin and Tom T. Hall. There are 3000 reserved tickets for each show which can be booked up months in advance from The Grand Ole Opry Ticket Office, 2800 Opryland Drive, Nashville, Tennessee 37214, (615) 889-3060. 1400 general admission tickets go on sale each Tuesday prior to the performance and can only be bought from the ticket office.

Despite the enormous number of musicians in town, the live music scene in Nashville is not particularly active. Most of the music is confined to the recording studios. What live country action there is can be found in Printer's Alley, a collection of restaurants and clubs that are often expensive. Here you'll find Boots Randolph's Club, George Jones' Possum Holler and the Carousel Club where popular Canadian singer and entertainer Ronnie Prophet is the host.

Years ago Nashville was noted for its small out-of-the-way clubs, where musicians picked and played in rustic interiors after a hard day at the studio. These clubs are fast disappearing though the Nashville Bluegrass Inn claims to be continuing the tradition. An unknown but competent bunch of bluegrass pickers play here from Wednesday to Saturday. The club is located at the rear of 1914 Broadway.

Across the river from the downtown area is the Dusty Road Tavern, 114 Woodland Street, a funky little roadhouse which features live bluegrass and country every night. Entertainment here is often of a "spontaneous nature" and I'm told that many pickers come here to unwind.

The heart of Nashville night life is down at Elliston Place. This is where the music business people come to relax. The Goldrush Bar is a very popular drinking spot and the place where you're most likely to see people like Buddy Emmons, Tracy Nelson, and other Nashville residents. Across the street is the city's showcase club The Exit/In which features all kinds of music from jazz, rock and blues through to occasional country.

If you have the stamina, the best time to come to Nashville is early June for the Country Music Fan Fare. "A fabulous fun-filled week featuring over 20 hours of stage shows with many country stars." There's also a bluegrass concert, square dancing, autograph parties, the Grand Master's Fiddling Championship, exhibitions by the major record companies and other special events. Write for full details to Fan Fair, PO Box 2138, Nashville, Tenn. 37214.

NEW ORLEANS, LOUISIANA

The historic and picturesque harbor town of New Orleans in Louisiana has a combination of rich musical elements, brought originally by the early settlers from Europe and Africa and kept alive in a cosmopolitan atmosphere that makes the place very special. New Orleans can claim to have been behind much of the best music that ever happened—jazz, rhythm and blues, rock 'n' roll and reggae.

Music can be found in great abundance in the city—there are dozens of clubs and bars featuring live bands and, with music a necessity at most public gatherings and parades, there's lots to be heard in the streets and parks as well. There are many talented local musicians and, for the fan prepared to search a little off the beaten track, the range of styles to be found is as great as in any other American city—jazz of many kinds, country, bluegrass, Cajun, zydeco (the music of the black Cajuns), ragtime, soul, rhythm and blues and modern rock.

For most music fans the name New Orleans inevitably brings to mind the loose, spontaneous sounds of twenties jazz and the names of King Oliver, Sidney Bechet, Jelly Roll Morton and the New Orleans Rhythm Kings. The good-time sounds of New Orleans traditional jazz can still be heard, recreated nightly at several clubs and at Preservation Hall. When the jazz stopped in the forties, rhythm and blues of an equally joyous and spontaneous nature took over and New Orleans music came to mean the sound of Professor Longhair, Smiley Lewis, Lloyd Price, Archibald and Fats Domino.

Though many of the R&B greats of the forties and fifties are either dead or retired there are still quite a few performing on a regular basis and it should be possible, even on a brief trip, to catch some famous names from the past like Lee Dorsey (remember his hits like "Ride Your Pony" and "Working In a Coalmine"?), Irma Thomas and Earl King. Friends of the legendary "godfather" of the New Orleans musicians, Professor Longhair, have opened a fine club called Tipitina's which is probably the best place to see R&B performers.

There isn't a great deal of orthodox contemporary music to be heard from the city's talented local musicians, instead they've developed styles from the past and taken them in new directions. Several young rhythm and blues musicians show strong reggae influences, which is ironic as it was New Orleans records of the fifties, broadcast over powerful clear channel radio stations to the West Indies, that helped form the basis for the blue beat and ska styles that were the musical predecessors of reggae. Like some good wines that do not travel well, Louisiana's home grown music of the eighties is popular locally but hasn't been well received elsewhere—in the past ten years only one local act (Louisiana's Le Roux) has achieved any kind of national fame.

The best time for music enthusiasts to visit New Orleans is in late April for the annual Jazz and Heritage Festival, a celebration of the culture of the city and the surrounding area. There's a special emphasis on music and food and the event is fast replacing Mardi Gras as the city's greatest celebration.

There are two overlapping parts of the festival—evening concerts and the Heritage Fair. The concerts feature big names in R&B, sophisticated jazz, gospel and traditional jazz, and are held at the Municipal Auditorium, The Mardi Gras Ballroom and on a steamer called The Admiral. The last named revives the New Orleans tradition of bands playing as a boat full of revelers journey lazily up and down the mighty Mississippi River.

The Heritage Fair takes place on weekends (Friday to Sunday from 11 AM to 7PM) on the infield of the Fair Grounds Race Track, one of the oldest and most beautiful horse racing tracks in the South. It's just a five-minute drive from the French Quarter at 1752 Gentilly Boulevard, near Esplanade Avenue and Broad Street. The Fair features music on several stages simultaneously and includes jazz, R&B, Cajun, blues, folk, Latin, gospel, country and bluegrass. The performers are among America's finest; guests in the past have included Muddy Waters, B.B. King, Irma Thomas, Bobby Bland, Clifton Chenier and Rocking Dopsie and his Cajun Twisters.

The clubs in the town become involved with the Festival and have extra shows and after-hours parties. This is easily the best time to see the cream of local talent with many of the older artists only appearing at this event. It's definitely a contender for "America's best festival." New Orleans is famous for its food and the festival offers the chance for you to try it all—gumbo, jambalaya, stuffed crabs, red beans and rice, and oyster po' boys. There are also displays of Louisiana crafts including the making of Louisiana accordians. Festival information from PO Box 2530, New Orleans,

Louisiana 70176.

Mardi Gras is New Orleans' best known public celebration and features plenty of music in the parades and as incidental special events in the clubs. Celebrated in the earliest Spanish and French settlements it first developed ito a street event in 1827. For most tourists it's the parades of brightly colored floats through the French quarter on Fat (Shrove) Tuesday that are Mardi Gras. The music is provided by high school and college marching bands.

People prepared to travel a little further afield from the center of the city can experience a number of interesting events including those featuring the Mardi Gras Indians. Because Blacks and American Indians in Louisiana were equally oppressed they founded an alliance with one another and created a solid bond. Mardi Gras Indians are direct descendants of the inter-racial marriages that evolved from that alliance. The Wild Tchoupitoulas (who've made a fascinating, strongly rhythm and blues influenced album for Island Records) are one of the tribes who parade more than 20 miles through the streets of New Orleans' 13th ward dressed in gaudy costumes and wearing huge feather headdresses, with hordes of "second liners" joining in the festivities.

New Orleans has many clubs, too many to mention, but this guide includes many of the best and will set you in the right direction for the rest. Be warned that several of the clubs in the French Quarter are rip-off joints featuring strip-tease or bad jazz—you'd be well advised to listen outside a club to the music first and to be wary of over-enthusiastic doormen trying to tempt you in. A walk down Bourbon Street, in the heart of the French Quarter, is recommended for a diverting—and free—taste of the area. Without actually entering any of the clubs you can hear a range of music and, through open doors, watch the strippers. The best view is from the middle of the street—motor traffic is fortunately stopped after dark!

A weekly paper called *Figaro* offers the best guide to what's on while two other papers, *Gris Gris* (which is published in Baton Rouge but covers the New Orleans scene in some detail) and *The Courier* are also worth checking out. The daily newspaper *The States-Item* lists some musical events in its entertainment section.

CLUBS

Tipitina's, 501 Napoleon, 899-9114. Away from the tourist area, the "real thing" in New Orleans music. Not to be missed. Named after the 1954 recording by Professor Longhair, the club features local acts like Snooks Eaglin, The Neville Brothers, The Dixie Kups, Bobby Mitchell, Earl King and many more. These days Earl plays with The Radiators, one of the few young groups projecting the true New Orleans funk rhythm sound. They are a "must see" group, as are the eclectic Li'l Queenie and the Percolators who formed virtually on stage at Tipitina's. Cover varies with act. The bar has an astonishingly wide range of non-alcoholic drinks. The jukebox is excellent—nearly all good reggae selections.

Jed's, 8301 Oak, 861-2585. Another club that's highly recommended. The best local R&B acts and occasional nationally known talent. Very good sight lines to the stage.

Ole Man River's, 2125 Highway 90 West, Avondale, 436-4000. "Keeps the music rollin' along." Great showcase club that's some way out of town, so you'll need your own transport.

Dream Palace, 534 Frenchman, 945-9409. Local R&B talent and occasional Chicago blues. A good place to see The Radiators.

Maple Leaf Bar, 8316 Oak, 866-9359. Across the road from Jed's (see above), this place has a good-time bar-room atmosphere with a pleasing variety of local acts including Kurt Kasson and the Wheeler Sisters, a jazz swing vocal group.

Blue Room, in the Fairmont Hotel, 529-7111. Name song stylists. Two performances a night. Cover from $12.

Le Club, in the Hyatt Regency Hotel, 561-1234. Top notch jazz spot. Three sets nightly from 9 PM. $8 plus cover includes a couple of drinks.

Jimmy's, 8200 Willow, 866-9549. Interesting and varied musical fare includes jazz, blues and R&B.

Duke's Place, atop the Monteleone Hotel, 581-1567. Dukes of Dixieland every night.

The Natchez, Toulouse Street Wharf at Jackson Sq., 524-9787. Every Saturday at 10PM there's a cruise down the Mississippi River with music from a New Orleans R&B artist or group. Can be expensive but worth every penny. Tickets from Mushroom Records or the wharf itself.

The President, foot of Canal St. Another steamer with musical trips every Saturday night. The steamboat boards at 8PM, sails at 9 and docks at midnight.

Preservation Hall, 726 St. Peter St., 523-8939. Traditional New Orleans jazz from 8:30 to 12:30. No alcohol.

Al Hirt's, 501 Bourbon. Jazz place.

Pete Fountain's, 800 Bourbon. Jazz place.

Lucky Pierre's, 735 Bourbon. Frankie Ford of "Sea Cruise" fame plays here regularly.

La Strada, 440 Bourbon. Through the open door you can hear Clarence "Frogman" Henry doing a medley of his old hits. Once inside it'll cost you over $6 for the first couple of drinks.

Eddie Bo's El Grande Lounge, 1218 N. Broad, 822-9948. Live music from R&B performers every Sunday in a club owned by "Check Mr Popeye" himself, though he can rarely be persuaded to perform.

Second Line, 1101 N. Rampart, 522-9578. Modern jazz spot that was previously the Vienna Room and before that a local R&B hangout called Lu and Charlie's.

Cajun Bandstand, 1822 Airline Hwy., five minutes from Kenner Airport, 729-8874. This is the best place around New Orleans to hear authentic Cajun music. Call for details of their weekend music events.

RECORD SHOPS

Memory Lane Records, 6417 Airline Hwy., Airline Park Shopping Center, Metairie, 733-2120. Godon Desoto's record store is out of the way but well worth a visit from R&B fans. Gordon loves New

Orleans music and has large stocks. He also arranges occasional concerts at the Harahan Lions Club, 10001 Hickory Ave., which he calls "Memory Lane Oldies But Goodies Dances" and feature artists like Tommy Ridgley and the Untouchables, Eddie Bo and the Jokers and Al Johnson.

Goldmine Records, 6469 Jefferson Hwy., Harahan Lane.

Russell's Rare Records, 1837 Magazine. Large stocks of New Orleans R&B, but be prepared to pay a lot—I've had several reports that many records here are expensive.

Mushroom Records on Broadway. "Helpful people and nice prices."

Leisure Landing, 4133 St. Charles. Large stocks of jazz records.

Cajun Bandstand, 1822 Airline Hwy., 5 minutes from Kenner Airport, 729-8874. Cajun records and paraphernalia. Live Cajun music on weekends—see club listings.

MUSEUM

New Orleans Jazz Museum, 833 Conti St., 525-3760. Closed Sundays. Instruments and memorabilia used by famous jazz musicians.

BACKGROUND READING

Walking To New Orleans by John Broven (Flyright, 18 Endwell Road, Bexhill-on-Sea, East Susex, England) retitled and amended in the US as *Rhythm and Blues in New Orleans* (Pelican Publishing). An essential book for anyone interested in the music of New Orleans. Broven, an Englishman, traces the development of New Orleans R&B through interviews with artists and carefully researched discographies.

Baton Rouge and beyond

If you're in New Orleans for more than a few days and have access to a car, take a trip out into the Louisiana countryside. Take the interesting levee road to Baton Rouge and pick up a copy of the local paper *Gris Gris* which will inform you of any interesting musical happenings. Kingfish, Perkins Rd., in Southdowns Shopping Center is a showcase club with an imaginative booking policy (call 343-0148 for information). Louisiana Cajun Country is worth exploring (see next chapter), but do make sure you visit on a weekend because nothing happens during the week. If you find yourself near Cankton, a very small place on Highway 93, don't fail to visit Jay's Lounge and Cockpit. The club calls itself "the last honky tonk," has T-shirts to prove it, and features some of the most danceable country and R&B bands in the South. You can be guaranteed an unforgetable night's entertainment and some of the best dancing you'll see anywhere. Next door is the cockpit where Mexican and Cajun farmworkers have been gambling over fighting cocks for years. $1 gets you in but outsiders aren't particularly welcome. The band is served with Cock Gumbo (featuring the evening's losers) after their gig.

(Special thanks to *Jon Newlin*, *Tad Jones*, *Lesley Stanford* and *Maureen MacMillan*)

CAJUN COUNTRY

Cajun Country is in southern Louisiana, a small area of flat farming country dotted with small towns that spreads maybe 100 miles from Lafayette in the east to Lake Charles in the west and is no more than 50 miles deep. It's inhabited by people whose roots stretch back to the fields of northern France, to Picardy and Normandy. From these provinces came the settlers that colonized what we know as Nova Scotia. They landed there in 1604 and called it Acadia. There they thrived until the conquest of French Canada by the British in the 18th century whereupon, because of their refusal to swear allegiance to the British Crown, they were deported to Louisiana, the last remaining French colony in North America.

Here they settled in the backwoods around the bayous of Teche and Courtableau among the Opelousa Indians. Eventually the US government bought Louisiana from the French and the Acadians became American. They have, however, always resisted Americanization and remain today a distinct minority group. Their Catholicism, their language and their strangely haunting music have combined to keep their culture separate and alive.

The Acadians should not be confused with the Creole population, the other French-speaking group in Louisiana, for the Creoles were the original settlers and their greatest concentration is in the eastern half of the state around New Orleans and Baton Rouge.

Cajun music is the sound of accordians and fiddles and songs sung in a weird patois French. The older styles don't use drums or guitar, the rhythm is supplied by triangle or a rubboard banged with spoons. Contemporary Cajun musicians add electric guitar, drums and steel to the accordian and fiddle. Cajun music is dance music, and in the many bars in this area you can experience the rowdy and boisterous atmosphere of a Fais Do Do, with young and old shouting and dancing the two-steps and breakdowns.

According to Tony Russell, traditional styles of Cajun music can still be found. "In the clutch of towns in the east—Opelousas and Ville Platte, Eunice and Basile, Crowley and Rayne (the Frog Capital of the World), Kaplan and Abbeville—are the country dancehalls, the lounges and cafes, where music of a more old fashioned cut can sometimes be heard."

Modern Cajun music is now a hybrid, containing elements of jazz, blues, French and German music, and country. Acadians have been slow to change their way of life, but have always been quick to draw on the popular sounds around them, being very conscious of the non-Cajun entertainers who've entered French homes and bars via the record player, TV and juke box. The more modern, citified sounds can be heard to the west and on into Texas, not Cajun country anymore, but where the music and bands are popular.

A number of black musicians have taken up Cajun music, and in their hands the sounds have been blended with a more commonplace rhythm and blues structure to produce zydeco—accordian blues—perhaps best exemplified by Clifton Chenier or Good Rocking Dopsie and his Cajun Twisters, the most popular black accordionists in the Cajun belt.

Going to Louisiana and finding Cajun music is very different from exploring other music scenes as this is somewhat uncharted territory and not easily accessible to the outsider. The people in the area who aren't of French descent are usually blissfully unaware of the music and where it can be found. Cajun clubs rarely need to advertise and are housed in remarkably ordinary looking buildings. Ask for help in shops with French names, like Hot Boudin, the excellent Cajun bakers in Henderson. It should be noted that the term "Cajun" should be used discreetly in Louisiana—much safer to say "French." Anthony Wall visited the state in search of traditional Cajun music and points out that it is essential to have your own transport. "We were in an area defined by Lafayette to the east, Eunice to the west, Abbeville to the south and Ville Platte to the north. We found people only too willing to help, and enthusiastic and appreciative that we wanted to hear authentic French music. It probably won't be advertized in the local papers, but just go into the record shops and bars and ask if there are any bands playing in town.

"It's difficult to miss it on Friday, Saturday and Sunday nights, especially Saturdays. During the week all these plain little towns seem as dull as Normandy. The week is for work and the weekend is for letting go, especially if it's festival weekend. Southern Louisiana abounds in festivals—dairy, swine, frog, crawfish and others. We went to a festival in Crowley that had rice eating and accordian contests. Unfortunately we missed the rice eating but it must have been quite something if the eaters were as good as the accordionists. The contest took place on a stage at the end of the street. Competitors, who ranged from youth to near-senility, had to play a two-step and a waltz and the standard was high. The judges were screened off to prevent them from recognizing the contestants. All the people looked so Gallic and conversation all around was in French, it seemed amazing that this was a part of America. When the results were announced, first and second place went to two sons of the late Iry LeJeune, perhaps the most famous of all Cajun accordian players. It seemed appropriate that his sons should be carrying it on."

The Cajun record industry has always been local, the two most important companies being Eddie Shuler's Goldband label in Lake Charles and Swallow which is run by Floyd Soileau in Ville Platte (Flat Town). Outside of Louisiana it's easier to get Cajun records in Europe than in America. The European Sonet label has issued excellent albums by traditional Cajun performers, like The Balfa Brothers and Nathan Abshire, and zydeco artists Clifton Chenier and Rocking Dopsie. With luck you can hear Cajun music on the radio. Stations in Crowley (KSIG 1450AM) and Eunice (KEUN) broadcast Cajun programs at weekends.

WHERE TO HEAR LIVE CAJUN MUSIC

Friday night:

Cajun Club, Highway 14 between Abbeville and Kaplan.

Bluegoose, Eunice.

Sissy's Lounge, Moss St., Lafayette. Small club.

Saturday morning:

You can experience one of the most unusual radio programs in the world on KEUN. It's broadcast live from Fred's Lounge on the corner of 6th Street and Chestnut in Mamou. You can experience this show live! Arrive about 9AM (when the live music starts), say hello to Revon Reed, the moderator, once your eyes become accustomed to the extreme darkness of the windowless bar, grab a beer for breakfast and settle back to enjoy the Cajun music that has been broadcast from this bar for years. "Relaxed madness!"

Saturday evening:

Bearcat Lounge on 190 West, Basile.

Webb's Lounge, Moss St., Lafayette. Highly recommended.

Lakeview Club, Mamou Rd., Eunice.

Triangle Club, Sunset Rd., Scott.

Town and Country Club, Riceville.

Cajun Club, Highway 14 between Abbeville and Kaplan.

La Poussiere Henderson Rd., Breaux Bridge.

B. Pellerin, Ducson.

The Happy Landing, Arnaudville Richard's, Lewisburg.

Snooks, Ville Platte.

Allen Fontenot's, Kenner.

The Belvedere, Rayne.

Bourque's, Lewisburg.

Sunday afternoon:

Triangle Club, Scott.

Sunday evening:

Boo Boo's, Breaux Bridge Road between Lafayette and Breaux Bridge.

WHERE TO HEAR LIVE ZYDECO MUSIC

Bon Tom Ruley, Lafayette. The home base of Rocking Dopsie and his Twister. Lafayette's number two zydeco band.

Dipsy Doodle, Breaux Bridge. Clifton Chenier plays here often.

Savoy's Music Center, Eunice. Home of Marc Savoy, leading maker of the Acadian accordion. If you hang around long enough a jam session will happen.

Chenier's Bar B Que, Lake Charles. Home of Morris (Big) Chenier, Clifton's uncle and a hot zydeco fiddler. The club is on Enterprise Street.

gris gris

JIN

La GAZETTE
des Acadiens

NEW YORK CITY, NEW YORK

New York is a fantastic city and well worth a visit. There's a thriving music scene offering something for everyone nearly every night of the week. Record collectors will be astonished at the number of record shops stacked high with rare and out-of-print discs. You can find almost any record you might want here but will probably have to pay a lot because New York dealers have high overheads and know the value of their stock.

The chance of a visit shouldn't be turned down though you'd be unwise to stay for long because everything, except public transport, is expensive and more than a few sessions in the clubs or record stores will eat up all your hard earned cash. A short, sharp visit packing in as much as is humanly possible — you'll find you need far less sleep than normal — is the best way to experience the place. Spring, early summer or autumn are the best times to visit, July and August should be avoided because of the heat and humidity that can make a stay, especially in a cheap hotel with no air conditioning, intolerable.

New York has become the most cosmopolitan city in the world with Italians, Germans, Poles, West Indians, Puerto Ricans and Chinese living in their own often clearly defined little areas. The romantic notion of a cultural "melting pot" is largely nonsense; it's much more like a blast furnace where anything can happen. Depending on who you are, what you do and what you have, this can be anything from the best to the worst place on earth. Within the space of only a few blocks you can witness the extremes of poverty and misery of drug addicts in Harlem to the ultra-fashionable activities of the hip-wealthy on the Upper East Side.

Visitors will see little of the seamy side of the city unless they actively seek it out. New York's reputation as a very dangerous place is unfair though you'd be advised to be alert and try not to look lost, innocent or naive (even if you are).

New York comprises five boroughs — Queens, Brooklyn, the Bronx, Staten Island and Manhattan — the last, the famous little island at the mouth of the Hudson River is where most of the musical action is to be found and where you'd be advised to stay. Manhattan is compact and surprisingly easy to explore, especially on foot. Avenues run north-south and streets east-west. Street numbers start low in the south and progress higher to the north. Most avenues and all principal streets have bus lines. Three subway lines link all the boroughs except Staten Island, the lines only connect at certain stations and finding your way around is akin to being in a very complicated maze — try to get a map. Trains run all night, though traveling around Manhattan after midnight can be dangerous.

Many of the best known New York clubs are in Greenwich Village in Manhattan, though with this area becoming more and more tourist orientated and inevitably more expensive, many New Yorkers now go to the newer places in SoHo — south of Houston Street. Here there are dozens of reasonably priced clubs and eating houses and if you're on a tight budget this is the place to come. You won't find many famous names but much of the music here is very good.

Clubs often stay open until 4AM, especially at weekends. At the better known places prices are expensive with the cost of drinks often going up after 10PM. It's useful to know that at several clubs you can perch on a bar stool and listen to the music for the price of a beer rather than pay the hefty cover charge for the privilege of sitting at a table — I always find this much easier to do if I'm on my own.

Some of the most innovative and exciting rock music of the seventies came from New York; from the Mercer Arts Center — arguably the birthplace of punk rock and now closed — Max's Kansas City and CBGB's. These last two clubs still feature modern rock bands but are very tourist orientated and most New York rock fans will be found at the newer clubs like Hurrah and Club 57. The modern rock scene in New York is comparable with the disco scene for its fickle support of the latest-in-place. It's impossible to tell which will be the next trendy spot; you'll have to check on arrival at one of the hipper record stores.

New York has a very strong jazz scene which is dealt with in the next chapter, but there are no nightspots specifically for the blues and soul fan. There is little live music in Harlem any more though the famous Apollo Theater has occasional shows. Name rhythm and blues performers turn up frequently, often in unlikely places like Max's Kansas City. Check the *Village Voice* and *New Yorker* listings carefully and you could well find a favorite blues or R&B singer performing somewhere in the city.

HONKY TONKIN'

Until the last few years country music was considered socially "unsuitable" for the sophisticated New Yorkers and anyone unfortunate enough to like the music tended to hide their records in the closet to avoid being embarrassed by their friends. All this has changed, several country music stars have played to packed houses at the city's biggest halls and there are clubs devoted to the music. The Bluegrass Club of New York publishes a monthly newsletter which is full of information about country music and bluegrass events. Send a stamped addressed envelope for a free copy to Box 1B, 417 East 89th Street, New York 10028 or phone 427-1488.

There's a mass of newsprint available in New York telling you about what's on. The Sunday edition of the *New York Times* has at at least 12 different sections, weighs in at over three pounds and is probably the greatest unread newspaper in the world — check the "Arts and Leisure" section for music listings. The most up-to-date information on the music scene can probably be found in the *Village Voice* which appears every Wednesday. It provides one of the best reads in the city with some of the finest music writers in America contributing. *The Soho News* is another weekly that has a good coverage of the music scene. *The New York Rocker* covers the new wave scene well but isn't good at listing clubs or gigs. *Cue* is a weekly glossy particularly useful for finding out which are the hip new discos. *The New Yorker* has an excellent coverage of jazz and some of the better-known rock spots. Anyone venturing into New Jersey should pick up a copy of the informative weekly *The Aquarian*.

A new book "dedicated to the resurgence of live music in New York City" is now available. *Steppin' Out — A Guide to Live Music in Manhattan* by Susanne Weil and Barry Singer (East Woods Press) covers over 150 places where musicians perform regularly.

The biggest rock showplace in New York is Madison Square Gardens, a 20,000-capacity arena. To be booked into Madison Square Gardens and then to sell out is to have made it in the music business. This isn't the best place to hear music but it remains very popular — a place to pay homage to your favorite rock star or band rather than to see and hear a good show. Smaller, and more suitable for seeing and hearing big name performers, are the Palladium on East 14th Street which has concerts most weeks, Felt Forum (the little brother of Madison Square Gardens and situated in the same block), Carnegie Hall, the Beacon Theater and Avery Fisher Hall.

One of the world's best known Black music showplaces is the Apollo Theater on West 125th Street in Harlem. Originally Hurtig and Seamon's Burlesque, it featured Yiddish entertainers like Fannie Brice and Sophie Tucker. In the thirties, as the black community of Harlem expanded downtown, it became a showcase for blues, jazz and subsequently R&B talent. Nearly all the great black musicians and singers, from Bessie Smith, Duke Ellington, Count Basie and Ella Fitzgerald to Aretha Franklin and Otis Redding, played here. The theater was closed for a time in the seventies after a serious shooting in the lobby and things have never been the same since, but there are occasional concerts by big name soul and disco acts and Amateur Nights on some Fridays.

The real musical action in New York takes place in the clubs. What follows is a selection, beginning with some of the best known.

CLUBS

Bottom Line, 15 W. 4th St., at Mercer St., 228-6300. Popular and crowded Greenwich Village showcase club close to Washington Square Park which plays host to some of the best acts in the business — folk, rock, blues, soul and country music. "One of the most comfortable places to play, or watch someone play, in the country." A place where music matters and is the all-important reason for being there — waitress service stops while the band or singer is on stage. Good sound and sight lines. Seats 450, cover from $5 and reservations are advisable — box office open from noon. Two shows a night.

The Other End, 149 Bleecker St., 673-7030. Formerly the Bitter End, a club with strong associations with the Greenwich Village folk boom of the sixties, it now features a wider range of music though folk styles, from the likes of Tom Paxton and Vassar Clements, are still the most regularly featured. The club now has a liquor license but has retained many of the best aspects of the Bitter End days including the intimate atmosphere and the unpretentious brick walls. Capacity 200, music charge from $3 with an additional $2.50 food and drink minimum. Shows at 9 and 11:30, but 9 and midnight on Friday and Saturday.

Lone Star Cafe, 61 Fifth Ave., at 13th St., 242-1664. You learn to expect the unexpected in New York and it was soon after seeing a man skateboarding down the middle of Fifth Avenue wearing a gasmask that I first stumbled upon a club that resembles the set of a Randolph Scott cowboy movie. The Lone Star Cafe is a little bit of Texas in the Big Apple complete with Lone Star beer and authentic Texan chili. The owners bring in the best musicians from the South — mainly progressive country artists but also blues singers like Bo Diddley and John Lee Hooker. Sound and sight lines are poor in parts of the downstairs area — try to get a table upstairs — but the club is an experience in itself and well worth a visit. Cover varies with act. Music nightly from 9 to 3.

CBGB's, 315 Bowery at Bleecker St., 982-4052. This was once a country music spot and the initials CBGB & OMFUG above the front door actually stand for "Country BlueGrass Blues and Other Music For Urban Gormandisers," but owner Harvey Kristal found that the location — in the Bowery, New York's skid row — was more suited to the needs of the small clique of emerging new wave rockers. Modern rock music is still the order of the day but New York rock fans insist the club is long past its best days. You can occasionally find other music — Screaming Jay Hawkins once made an unforgettable appearance here.

Max's Kansas City, 213 Park Ave. S. at 17th St., 777-7870. Like CBGB's, the nightspot features American and sometimes British new wave rockers. "A faded glitter palace." Most of the customers seem to be tourists.

Hurrah, 36 W. 62nd St., 541-4909. One of the most comfortable places to hear new rock music in New York. A successful, pioneering combination of rock disco — intelligent selection of modern rock sounds played over excellent sound system — and live music spot.

Club 57, Irving Plaza, 17 Irving Pl., at E. 15th St., 475-9671. Club 57 was a little 120-capacity club in St. Mark's Place that couldn't accommodate everyone who wanted to visit so began hiring the Irving Plaza, a Polish-American ballroom with ornate chandeliers. Now a very popular weekend spot for new wave rock music.

The Rocker Room, 1 E. 48th St., 755-4990. During the week this is an undistinguished bar called Nemo's but it becomes a popular rock music venue each weekend.

Reno Sweeney, 126 W. 13th St., 691-0900. Expensive, but one of the best cabaret spots in New York. Shows at 9 and 11:30. Admission varies with artist.

City Limits, Seventh Ave. S. at 10th St., 243-2242. Country music place. Energetic bands play every night from 10 — dancing is encouraged.

O'Lunney's, 915 Second Ave. near 48th St., 751-5470. Great little country music place that features country talent from the Northeast including Them Fargo Brothers and Chuck McDermott. Good jukebox.

Trax, 100 W. 72nd St. near Columbus Ave., 799-1448. Music business hangout which showcases up-and-coming new talent. Capacity 280, cover from $4. Closed Sundays.

Great Gildersleeves, 331 Bowery between 2nd and 3rd Sts., 533-3940. Local rock and occasional name bands.

Kenny's Castaway, 157 Bleecker St., 473-9870 or 473-9871. Singer/songwriter, occasional bands and blues singers.

Folk City, 130 W. 3rd St. at Sixth Ave., 254-8449. Long established folk club where many now famous singers started out.

Broadway Charly's, 813 Broadway between 11th and 12th Sts., 473-8805.

RECORD SHOPS

Record collectors should start with a copy of the New York Yellow Pages and check the long lists of specialist record stores. Many are in the Greenwich Village area and, given time and vast quantities of money, you should be able to find virtually everything you've ever wanted!

Farfel's Records, 179 W. 4th St., between Sixth and Seventh Aves., 675-4126. Housed in a basement so look carefully for their "Music Inn" sign. "They specialize in rare LPs and 45s — rock, jazz, R&B and soundtracks. Lots of rare Presley items. English records from the sixties at fantastic prices so this could be a good place for English collectors to bring their unwanted records."

Bleecker Bob's Golden Oldies, 179 McDougal St., off W. 8th St., 475-9677. Open daily from noon to midnight. Good selection of obscure R&B is hidden away round the corner, main sales here seem to be of British rock items.

Discophile, 26 W. 8th St., 473-1902. Very good for new wave rock and local labels. Good place to ask about the best new rock bands and hip nightspots.

Happy Tunes, 53 W. 8th St., 475-6580. Lots of cut-outs at good prices.

Dayton's, 824 Broadway, corner of 12th St., AL4-5084. Old/rare records are expensive, but they sell new albums at very reasonable prices.

Second Hand Rose, 525 Sixth Ave., 675-3735. "One of the best shops for nostalgia stuff that I've found. Gene and Shelli run a friendly, chaotic store, but with patience I unearthed some Rick Nelson Imperial and Decca originals in mint condition."

House of Oldies, 267 Bleecker St., 243-0500. "World headquarters for out of print 45s," they claim. They have thousands of 45s and if you send them your wants list (their zip code is 10014) they'll let you know how much it will cost. Catalogues are $2.

Record City, 734 Broadway, 982-5189. "Ask for Kenny, who's very knowledgeable about sixties music. There are literally thousands of singles — all unplayed — arranged alphabetically for $2 each. It would have taken a few days to get through them but I noticed original King and Ace singles. A very helpful and friendly place."

Downstairs Records, 55 W. 42nd St., 221-8989. In the subway arcade is a store that claims to carry "the largest selection of punk and new wave singles in mid-town Manhattan." The back room here is crowded with old singles at prices mostly under $5.

Record Hunter, 507 Fifth Ave., between 42nd and 43rd St., 697-8970. Oldies store that will try and get you anything you want.

Colony Record and Radio Center, 1619 Broadway at corner of 49th St., 265-2050. "Lots of obscure records that aren't too overpriced."

Free Being Record House, 129 Second Ave., 260-1774. Cheap promo and cut-out albums and a large selection of second hand records. "Very good value — I found the long-deleted Mother Earth album 'Make A Joyful Noise' here for $2.96."

Disco Mat Records, 714 Lexington Ave., 759-3777. Everything hugely discounted.

Matt Umanov's, 276 Bleecker St., 675-2157. Guitar shop in Greenwich Village — sells a small but well chosen selection of records.

Record Exchange, 842 Seventh Ave. Deals in out-of-print records.

K & B Records Inc., 118 E. 14th St. Recommended store that sells records, stereo equipment and instruments.

Sam Goody stores (there are several around the city) and the record departments of **Korvette's** carry large stocks of records and offer big discounts on selected new releases.

King Karol stores are more expensive but they have the largest stocks and if there is a particular record you are after, and it's still on catalogue, you'd be advised to come here first. The biggest store is at 126 W. 42nd St. at Sixth Ave., 354-6880. Other stores at 7 W. 48th St.; 1500 Broadway; 460 42nd St.; 940 Third Ave.; 1521 Third Ave.

RADIO

A sensible idea for visitors from abroad on your first night into New York (when you're jet-lagged and tired) is listening to the radio. Spin the dial and take your choice of over 50 stations. After a few days you'll realize that the programming is remarkably dull and unimaginative but on the first night this isn't going to bother you because flipping from station to station is such a novelty. You can play similar games with the TV, of course.

WNEW 102.7, WPLJ 95.5 and WPIX 101.9 are three of the best rock stations on the FM band, while WABC 770 AM plays the top pop hits of the day over and over again, WKTU 92.3 is the disco station that became hugely successful when it changed from a "mellow music" format in 1978 and WBLS 107.5 plays disco and soul and is one of America's slickest black stations. WHN 1050 AM is a country/MOR station that plays only proven hits though some evenings there are live broadcasts from the Lone Star Cafe. WINS 1010 AM was the first New York radio outlet to hire Alan Freed in the fifties — it's now all news. WMCA 570 AM was the former "Good Guys" station that was home to Murray the K who tagged it "the official Beatles station," but is not all telephone talk. WCBS 101.1FM has an oldies format.

JAZZ IN THE BIG APPLE

New York's Manhattan island is probably the best place in the world to hear live jazz because there is so much available. On many nights there is almost too much to choose from — music in all styles, from Dixieland to boogie-woogie, from swing to avant-garde, from the greatest names in the business to the most interesting up-and-coming new artists.

Jazz musicians are generally credited with having coined the expression "the Big Apple" to describe the city because there's always so much work available, always room for a talented musician to take another "bite." Lately jazz, which has always been popular in New York City, has picked up an even larger following than before. Where 15 years ago there were only a half-dozen clubs devoted exclusively to jazz, there are now over 40; and that doesn't include all the loft establishments that have sprung up over the last few years.

Peter Occhiogrosso, a New York journalist who's followed the movement from its earliest days, wrote about "loft jazz" in *Melody Maker*: "The label is something of a misnomer — initiated by the loft-owners in an attempt to bring attention to their underground venues — although it does adequately encapsulate a group of musicians from all over the US who've come to New York and created some of the most exciting new jazz in the decade since Coltrane's death. The lofts range from large open spaces with polished floors and stunning acoustics, such as Environ, to smaller, more intimate lofts like Jazzmania, which sports comfortable furniture, rugs on the floor and modestly priced refreshments." Most lofts do not have liquor licenses.

The Newport Jazz Festival is held in New York each year in late June and early July. It's probably the most prestigious jazz festival in the world. It was started over 25 years ago at Newport, Rhode Island, but moved to New York in 1972. The producer since the very first festival, George Wein, relies heavily on established jazz names but arranges enough concept and avant-garde programs to avoid any sense of predictability. For information call 787-2020.

Upcoming gigs are listed in a free fortnightly newsletter published by Jazz Interactions, 527 Madison Avenue, Suite 1615,

New York, NY 10022, Tel.: 688-8257, and available from the Times Square Information Center at 43rd and Broadway. *NYC/-Jazz*, published on the third Wednesday of every month, is a selective catalogue of jazz activity in the greater New York area. It costs 25¢ from newstands or from 436 West Broadway, New York, NY 10012. *NYC/Jazz* includes a map guide to clubs and a useful jazz radio schedule. For those of you who are eager to hear some good jazz but aren't very knowledgeable about who's who, you'd be well advised to check the "Goings On About Town" listings in the *New Yorker* magazine. They are very helpful in telling you about the artists playing and what to expect at different clubs. For up to the minute information ring Jazzline on (212) 421-3592 for a taped message of last minute changes and additions.

CLUBS

There are frequent big-name jazz concerts at the major halls already listed in the New York City chapter and also at the Public Theater, 425 Lafayette Street, 677-1750; Cami Hall, 165 West 57th Street, 582-4090; and the St. Charles Auditorium, 211 West 141st Street, 989-3220. The best places to hear jazz is in the clubs. The following list, though not comprehensive, does include most of the best.

Ali's Alley, 77 Greene St., 226-9042. SoHo loft that's more like a nightclub — liquor is available. Presents some of the very best experimental jazz in town. Live music starts around 10 PM.

Arthur's Tavern, 57 Grove St., 242-9468. Informal jazz spot with tacky furnishings. Singer/pianist Mabel Gordon plays Thursdays to Saturdays and is highly recommended.

Beefsteak Charlie's Jazz Emporium, 5th Ave. and 12th St., 675-7812. Local jazz talent at a branch of a popular steakhouse chain. Musicians sit close to the window and can be watched (though not heard) from the street.

Barbara's, 78 W. 3rd, 473-9326. Music nightly from 9:30.

Bradley's, 70 University Place at 11th St., 228-6440. Large, noisy club that features some of the best pianists and bassists in

American jazz. Music every night from 9:30. Clientele like talking during the music, which means it isn't always easy to hear the talented guests.

Peter Brown, 168 W. 96th St., 866-4710. A restaurant and supper club with live jazz nightly.

Broady's, 798 Columbus at 98th, 850-4400.

Clifford's 72nd Street Jazz, 151 W. 72nd St., 873-8586.

Carnegie Tavern, 165 W. 56th St., 757-9522. Pianist Ellis Larkins, who has accompanied Ella Fitzgerald, Joe Williams and Sylvia Syms among others, is a regular here.

Eddie Condon's, 144 W. 54th St., 265-8277. Traditional jazz and dinner every night until 3AM.

Cookery, 21 University Place at 8th St., 674-4450. Operated by Barney Josephson who ran the original Cafe Society. Blues and boogie-woogie from regulars like pianist Sammy Price and singer Alberta Hunter.

Crawdaddy, Vanderbilt Ave. at 45th St., 687-4450. Just like being in a club in the French Quarter of New Orleans. Creole food and Dixieland jazz. Closed weekends.

Drawing Room, 510 Greenwich St., 431-9478.

Eric, 1700 Second Ave., 534-8500.

Environ, 476 Broadway, 964-5190. Loft jazz place on the 11th floor. "Stunning acoustics."

Fat Tuesday's, 190 Third Ave. at 17th St., 533-7902. Basement jazz club with name talent.

Fortune Garden, 1160 Third Ave., 744-1212. Tuesday to Saturday evenings and on Sunday afternoon.

Gregory's, 1149 First Ave. at 63rd St., 371-2220. Genuine swing music in a very small bar. Music from Wednesday to Sunday from 10PM.

HONKY TONKIN'

Hopper's, 452 Sixth Ave. at 11th St., 262-0250. Name jazz talent. Two shows per night Mondays through Thursdays, three on weekends.

Jazzmania, 14th E. 23rd St. and Madison Ave., 477-3077. Relaxed, intimate jazz loft on the fourth floor. Jazz brunch on Sundays, 3 to 5PM.

Ladies Fort, 2 Bond St., 674-7960. Great loft jazz gathering spot.

La Chansonette, 890 Second Ave., PL2-7320. Easy listening jazz for dancing.

Michael's Pub, 211 E. 55th St., 753-2272. Popular jazz spot with interesting Tudor decor. Woody Allen often plays clarinet with a traditional New Orleans seven-piece band on Monday nights.

Mikell's, 760 Columbus Ave. at 97th St., 864-8832. Often crowded Upper Westside Jazz and soul cafe where the rhythm and blues sextet Stuff (featuring Cornell Dupree) was formed. Music from 10PM to 2AM.

Motivations, 476 Broome St., 226-2108.

One Fifth Avenue, Fifth Ave. at 8th St., 260-3434.

Pepper's, 19 East St. off Park Avenue, 260-3699.

Prescott's, 353 Greenwich St., 925-3545.

Red Blazer Too, 1516 Third Ave., 876-6350. "Live nostalgia jazz."

Jimmy Ryan's, 154 W. 54th St., 664-9700. Dixieland jazz. No cover or minimum.

Reno Sweeney, 126 W. 13th St., 691-0900. Cabaret club (see New York listings) has occasional jazz acts.

Seventh Avenue South, 21 Seventh Ave. at Leroy St., 242-4694. Casual club owned by the successful musicians Mike and Randy Brecker — the Brecker Brothers.

Storytowne, 41 E. 58th St., 755-1640. Name jazz talent in casual downstairs room. Cover from $6. Two sets a night, third on Saturday at 1AM.

Studio Rivbea, 24 Bond St., 777-8656.

Surf Maid, 151 Bleecker Street, 473-8845.

Sweet Basil, 88 Seventh Ave. S. at Bleecker St., 242-1785. Music every night from 10PM with name artists.

Tramp's, 125 E. 15th St., 260-0370. Variety of jazz talents with the emphasis on entertainment. Ragtime, blues and jazz here.

The Village Corner, 142 Bleecker St. at W. Broadway, 473-9762. Jazz pianists Lance Hayward and Jim Roberts are residents.

Village Gate, 160 Bleecker St., 475-5120. A popular Greenwich Village club which gets big name and blues acts.

Village Vanguard, 178 Seventh Ave. S., 255-4037. Top flight traditional jazz spot with star names. Cover from $5. According to the *New Yorker*, "the least pretentious and the most prestigious jazz club in town."

Tin Palace, 325 Bowery at 2nd St., 674-9115. Not far from the rock spot CBGB's. Good music in a relaxed atmosphere with an imaginative booking policy that attracts many off-duty musicians among the listeners. Music nightly from 10.

Sha Sha House, 338 W. 39th St., 736-7547. Jazz from South America and Africa. Tropical vegetarian food.

West End Cafe, 2911 Broadway at 113th St, 666-8750. Columbia University branch of the Jazz Hall of Fame. Old hangout of Jack

Kerouac and where William Borroughs wrote *Naked Lunch*. The music here is nearly all pre-fifties in origin. Music nightly from 9.

West Boondock, 114 Tenth Avenue at 17th St., 924-9723. Extraordinary-looking place as *The New Yorker* describes — "Convenient to a New York City truck route and not much else, this bar has red Afro-psychedelic walls, hundreds of gold Christmas tree ornaments hanging from the ceiling and a tiny (about five by ten feet) soul food kitchen. Other assets include sturdy, animated piano-bass duos that hold forth every night from 8 to 2."

St. Peter's Lutheran Church, 54th St. and Lexington Ave., 935-2200. Jazz Vespers every Sunday at 5PM.

RECORD SHOP

Record Hunter, 507 Fifth Ave. between 42nd and 43rd Sts., has large stocks of jazz albums.

RADIO

WRVR 106.7 FM, 6AM to midnight.

WNYC 93.9 FM, Saturday 4 to 5PM, Sunday 9:30 to 11PM.

WBAI 99.5 FM, Monday to Friday 10PM to midnight, Tuesday and Wednesday midnight to 5AM. Live jazz.

WRLB 107.1 FM, Sunday to Friday 10PM to midnight.

WEVD 97.9 FM, Monday to Friday 10PM to 1AM.

WKCR 89.9 FM, "Jazz Alternatives" 6 to 9PM, "Out To Lunch" noon to 3PM, "Jazz 'til Dawn" 2 to 6AM.

BOOKSTORE

The New Morning Bookstore, 169 Spring St., 966-2993. Jazz books.

OHIO

Cleveland

Cleveland, Ohio's biggest city, sprawls for over 40 miles along the shore of polluted Lake Erie. It isn't the most attractive of cities and Marvel Comics' hero Howard The Duck referred to it as "the armpit of the nation." With nearby Akron, Cleveland has produced a number of unusual and innovative new wave rock bands, like Devo and Pere Ubu, who've received lavish media praise in New York and London, yet have found little popular support at home.

Pere Ubu vocalist David Thomas explained to British journalist Paul Rambali, who'd been sent by *New Musical Express* to investigate the strange new sounds coming out of Ohio, "There's this relationship between machines and flesh in Cleveland that is very strange. It's a strong juxtaposition. Cleveland is a giant, blown-out factory town. There's the Flats with all this incredible industry, steel mills going flat out all day and all night, and it's just half a mile away from where all the people live. This gives them the feeling that there's no future for somebody here, and all the musicians seem to be in love with that fact."

Tracking down new Ohio bands in the Devo or Pere Ubu mould is very difficult; not particulary liked by the home town fans, they presumably work away in their private home-made studios until they're ready to send their tapes to people in New York and London. For details of the conventional music scene in town — and there's a lot going on at both a national and local talent level — check out the weekly newspaper *Scene*.

CLUBS

Hennessy's, 11729 Detroit Ave., Lakewood, 521-2636. A legendary rock music bar that David Bowie is alleged to have dubbed "the home of the stars" when he was here in 1972. Highlight of the year is the All-Star Cleveland Musicians' Jam held each Thanksgiving Eve.

Agora, E. 24th, 696-8333. Agora clubs have begun springing up in places as far away as Atlanta, Georgia. This is the original, a 900-seater showcase that features name talent.

Bobby McGee's, 1612 Euclid Ave., 687-1130. Cleveland's premier folk club with well-known names most Wednesdays.

Flipside, 3935 Mayfield, Cleveland Heights, 291-4272. Folk, rock and country. Regular Thursday night gigs feature bluesman Robert Jr. Lockwood. Recommended.

Coach House, 2025 Abbington, 791-3096. Near the Case-Western University on Cleveland's east side is a club with the area's only reggae jukebox. Live folk, blues and country bands.

Peabody Cafe, Cedar and Taylor, Cleveland Heights. Top names in jazz and blues featured here from time to time.

Pirates Cove, 1059 Old River Road, 241-0792. In the Flats area of downtown Cleveland — the best local rock bands are featured.

Painesville Agora, 54 State St. 25 miles east of downtown Cleveland another Agora showcase club, this time located in an old movie theater.

(Thanks to *Peanuts* of ***Scene***)

Akron

Akron is a normal Midwestern town in a state that's regarded as the most typical of the whole 50 and is often used by statisticians for just that reason. Not everything is normal though — it's produced a disproportionately large number of rock performers over the years from the Ohio Express, the Raspberries and the James Gang to Rachel Sweet and was at the forefront of the new wave rock era throwing up such odd bands as The Bizarros and Tin Huey. There's also the Cuyahoga River, which flows from Akron to Lake Erie, has been designated a major fire hazard, and was immortalized by Randy Newman in his song "Burn On, Big River."

CLUB

The Nightclub, 289 Darrow Rd., 733-7933. Dance bands on the weekends, national acts during the week — often jazz.

Columbus

A biweekly free paper called *Focus* is the best guide to live music in Columbus. Each summer there are Music In The Air concerts that cover a variety of musical genres and are free — information at 221-2000.

CLUBS

Agora, 1722 High St., 294-6251. Purpose-built rock spot has 3000 capacity and showcases nationally-known acts like Dr. Hook and Bonnie Raitt.

Zachariah's Red Eye Saloon, 1778 N. High St., 294-3386. Country and rock bands.

The Railroad, 251 Granville St., 475-2794. Jazz and rock.

PHILADELPHIA, PENNSYLVANIA

Music business people describe Philadelphia as an "important market" because its rock fans buy a lot of albums and concert tickets. They're also good at spotting and supporting new musical trends that are going to be big. Along with Boston and New York, this was one of the first American cities to encourage the new wave of British rock artists.

Philadelphia is noted for breaking new talent though not necessarily its own — local boys Todd Rundgren, Daryl Hall and John Oates had to leave town before they could find the pathway to success. The current lack of encouragement for local talent is a reversal of the way it was in the late 50s and early 60s when the nationally syndicated Dick Clark TV show "American Bandstand" gave local artists like Bobby Rydell, former chicken market employee Chubby Checker, and The Orlons enormous exposure and subsequent chart success with the local Cameo-Parkway record company.

The label folded in 1968 at about the same time that Kenny Gamble and Leon Huff were establishing their empire. They launched their own record company, Philadelphia International, in 1973 and it quickly became a source of creative soul music — from The O'Jays, Harold Melvin and the Bluenotes, etc. — though has now lost the dominance in the US soul charts it used to enjoy. Philadelphia is increasingly known for the sound of its session players and the quality of production at Sigma Sound.

The city has a strong folk music tradition. The Philadelphia Folksong Society at 7113 Emlen Street, CH7-1300, holds monthly concerts on board its boat on the Delaware River. Several clubs and bars feature jazz, though the city's well-known Arch Street club Just Jazz has closed. Ask at the excellent Third Street Jazz record shop for details of the best live jazz to be heard in town.

Two papers carry gig listings for Philadelphia — the New Jersey weekly *The Aquarian* and a free biweekly called *Old City Digest*. Major rock acts play at Fairmont Park, an open air stadium in the Robin Hood Dell; The Academy of Music; Tower Theater, a renovated movie house; the Spectrum, a large indoor arena; and the Shubert Theater.

CLUBS

Walnut Street Theater, 9th and Walnut Sts., 574-3550. New wave rock.

New Locust Theater, 1400-seat showcase club for top soul/R&B acts like Ashford and Simpson and Betty Wright.

Stars, 2nd and Bainbridge, 627-8033. 300-seat showcase club.

Bijou Cafe, 1409 Lombard St., L03-9284. Showcase club featuring up-and-coming rock groups and new recording artists. Expensive.

Hot Club, 21st and South Sts., 545-9370. New wave rock on weekends, occasional jazz during the week.

J.C. Dobbs, 3rd and South Sts., 922-8713. Local rock talent. One of several small clubs on South Street. Philadelphia pop group of the sixties The Orlons once had a hit that extolled the dubious virtues of "South Street."

The Main Point, 874 Lancaster Ave., Bryn Mawr, LA5-3375. Long established and highly respected venue in the Philadelphia suburbs. Wide range of good music — folk, new country and jazz. Nice place with nice people. Well worth a visit if you can get the transport from the center of town.

Guthrie's, 1116 Old York Road, Abington, 884-4407. Traditional folk, folk-rock and country blues featured in this club located about 12 miles from Philadelphia.

RECORD SHOPS

Third Street Jazz, 10 N. 3rd St., MA7-3366. Good place for those hard to find jazz albums — not particularly cheap but there are some amazing bargains in recent rock and country releases. They have enormous stocks of records that aren't displayed — try and persuade them to let you explore their cellar full of goodies!

Album Alley, 6325 Green St., 438-1826. Bob Gobson's shop is another highly recommended spot for record collectors.

HONKY TONKIN'

Platters, 1009 Chestnut, 923-6003. "Lots of cheap records."

Val Shively's, 69th St., Hovertown/Upper Darby. Take the subway to Upper 69th St. station in this suburb a few miles southwest of Philadelphia. No serious collector of obscure soul and R&B should miss this place. Enormous stocks and an excellent place to meet fellow collectors and exchange information about other sources of rare records.

SAN FRANCISCO, CALIFORNIA

Live music is thriving in San Francisco with several big names playing the concert halls, though generally it is the many small clubs that are putting on the best entertainment around the city — usually with a small cover charge, in a friendly atmosphere. Every night of the week it should be possible to find something, whatever your taste, from straight country music to avant garde jazz.

The city remains a stronghold for musicians and fans from the hippy days of the late sixties — The Grateful Dead and Jefferson Starship still call it home. Modern music has made more than a few ripples, there are some interesting new wave rock bands, and the city's huge gay population has played an important part in making this one of America's hottest disco cities. There's a healthy blues scene with an annual festival that's worth checking out if you're here in August.

San Francisco was the birthplace of free-form progressive radio that has since developed/degenerated into "hip easy listening" or AOR ("Album Orientated Rock"). It was begun at KMPX and then KSAN by a man named Tom Donahue, whose radical alternative to the radio domination of Top 40 stations in the mid-sixties was a loose-limbed, unstructured and laid-back format. KSAN 95 FM remains San Francisco's favorite rock station.

The city is located on a peninsula, making it very compact and easy to explore. Since most of the streets except Market are laid out on a grid pattern, it's relatively easy for the stranger to find his way around. Visitors without a car will find no problem here — like New York you either walk or take the excellent public transportation. San Francisco is supposed to be "everybody's favorite city" and it isn't difficult to see why. It has a beauty and sophistication that few places on earth can match and a sense of freedom that's made it particularly welcoming to nonconformists of all kinds.

Some of the clubs and the people who frequent them are stylish and smart. You may feel more comfortable heading east across the Bay Bridge to the University of California campus at Berkeley, once the center of American student unrest and protest but now calm, easy-going and a popular tourist attraction. The relaxed atmosphere of Berkeley makes a welcome change from San Francisco, and you'll find clubs and bars are generally cheaper and a lot more casual. There are several very good book and record stores — particularly strong on second-hand items.

Interesting places near San Francisco include Sausalito which can be reached by going across the Golden Gate Bridge — one of America's most spectacular man-made attractions and offering incomparable views of the city, the Bay, and infamous Alcatraz Island — or by ferry from the foot of Market Street. North of Sausalito is Marin Country, Bodega Bay (where Hitchcock made "The Birds") and the artists' colony of Mendocino.

Seventy miles south of San Francisco is Santa Cruz, home of the new University of California campus. The town lies at the edge of the beautiful Monterey Bay, and you can spend your days in the sun on the beach and nights in the innumerable clubs and bars listening to a diversified selection of music that ranges from the truly awful to the very good. A lot of places don't have cover charges, so you can wander around until you find something worth listening to.

Two papers cover the music scene for San Francisco and the surrounding area. Best for club listings is *The San Francisco Bay Guardian*, while the bi-monthly *BAM — The California Music Magazine* resembles *Rolling Stone* and runs lengthy features on worthy local bands.

CONCERT HALLS AND STADIUMS

San Francisco's best known rock place, Winterland (the ballroom where "The Last Waltz" film of The Band's final concert was made), has closed. Most of the big rock concerts in the area are held across the Bay in Oakland at either the Coliseum, the Stadium or the Paramount Theater.

SAN FRANCISCO CLUBS

Old Waldorf, 44 Battery St., between Clay and Washington, 397-3884. San Francisco's premier rock showcase club seats 600 and features some of the hottest acts of the day. Originally a small club in the downtown area, it moved to a new home in the heart of the business district in 1975. The club's bookers have a remarkable knack of spotting and booking acts just before they break into the big time. Two shows a night at 8:30 and 11:30.

Great American Music Hall, 859 O'Farrell, 885-0750. Lavishly decorated turn-of-the-century opera house (its former row seats now replaced by wooden tables and chairs) that features big names in rock, jazz and folk.

Mabuhay Gardens, 443 Broadway, 956-3315. San Francisco's main punk/new wave rock spot features mainly local talent. Shows at 11PM.

The Boarding House, 960 Bush, 441-4333. One time recording studio where Bing Crosby made "White Christmas" and now an ideal place to see singer/songwriters like local favorites John Stewart and Barry "The Fish" Melton.

Keystone Korner, 750 Vallejo, 781-0697. An excellent jazz spot. Name performers in a relaxed and intimate atmosphere. Two shows nightly at 9:30 and 11:30.

The Palms, 1406 Polk at Pine, 673-7771. An interesting and diverse selection of music from rock through gospel, blues through country. Recommended by several visitors to the city.

The Mocambo, Polk at Sutter, 776-2133. Trendy cabaret spot featuring jazz, soul and R&B.

Venetian Room, The Fairmont Hotel, California and Mason, 772-5163. Top notch supper club/cabaret. Proper dress required. Big name acts.

Coffee Gallery, 1353 Grant, 397-3751. Frequent blues and R&B talent. Zydeco favorites Queen Ida and her Bon Temps band are frequently here with their hot sound from the Louisiana bayous.

Last Day Saloon, 406 Clement, 387-6343. An interesting mixture of San Francisco talent with more than a fair sprinkling of country- and folk-influenced rock outfits.

Plowshares Coffee House, 312 Fort Mason Bldg. (third floor), near Laguna at Marina. Coffee house of the San Francisco Folk Music Club. Concerts every Sunday. Call 441-8901 for information. The

Folk Club is based at 885 Clayton and oversees folk music events in the city. It publishes a bi-monthly newsletter *The Folknic*.

SAN FRANCISCO RECORD, BOOK, AND ROCK MEMORABILIA SHOPS

Tower Records, Columbus and Bay (near The Wharf). One of the excellent Tower chain of stores in California — they carry an enormous and varied stock.

O'Farrell Records and Books, 439 O'Farrell, 776-1822. Collectors' records bought, sold or traded. Open Tues. through Sat. 1PM to 6PM.

American Music and Records Store, 2388 Mission, 647-2098. Specialists in Latin American music. Very good stocks of Tex-Mex.

Magic Flute, 510½ Frederick, 661-4257. Open noon to 7PM, closed Mondays. Many rare items at good, though not cheap, prices.

Recycled Records, 1415 Upper Grant Ave., North Beach, 982-5442 and at 1377 Haight at Masonic, 626-4075. Very good selection of new and used records including collectors' section.

Revolver Records, 520 Clement, 386-6128. Good selection of second-hand records.

Books and Records, 2222 Polk near Vallejo, 771-7909. Good for out-of-print records and books.

Bill Graham's, 1333 Columbus Ave., 673-4970. T-shirts, posters, postcards, handbills of Bill Graham concerts from the last decade.

City Lights, 261 Columbus Ave., 362-8193. Still there after 20 years — famous shop associated with Ginsberg and the Beats.

EAST BAY CLUBS

Freight and Salvage, 1827 San Pablo, Berkeley, 548-1761. Stronghold of local country, bluegrass and mountain music.

International Cafe, 2516 Telegraph, Berkeley, 841-9070. Local new wave rock talent and occasional blues from locals like Sonny Rhodes (who's strongly recommended).

Keystone Berkeley, 2119 University Ave., Berkeley, 841-9903. Showcase club featuring up-and-coming rock, country and folkish acts.

Michael's Den, 1110 10th St., Berkeley, 526-1974. Frequent reggae and calypso.

La Pena Center, 3105 Shattuck Ave., Berkeley, 849-2568. A Latin-American cultural center, with a great restaurant and live music several nights a week — blues, country, swing, Mexican, Japanese drumming.

Town House, 5862 Doyle, Emeryville, 658-2885. A one-time prohibition speakeasy, now a restaurant/bar with attractive rustic interior and appropriate country/folkish music from the likes of talented local Tom Russell.

Mr. Major's, 8021 MacArthur, Oakland, 569-6000. Jazz spot.

EAST BAY RECORD SHOPS, DISTRIBUTOR AND RECORD LABELS

Rather Ripped, 1878 Euclid Ave., Berkeley, 848-6495. A good place for "off the wall items." A shop that's dedicated to rock and roll outsiders. Trades old records for new.

Rasputin's, 2379 Telegraph Ave., Berkeley, 843-3908. Enormous place with large second-hand and cut-out sections.

Leopold's, at Telegraph and Durant, Berkeley. Large stocks of records, very reasonable prices.

Down Home Music, Inc., 10341 San Pablo Ave., El Cerrito, California 94530, (415) 525-1494. This address houses a record store, a record label, a record distributor and a film company that specializes in musical subjects. The whole complex is located in El Cerrito between Berkeley and Richmond.

Down Home Music is a record store open Wed. to Sat. 1PM to 7PM ("or call for an appointment or ring the buzzer and we will be glad to let you in if any of us are in the building"). The shop has a mail order service and issues periodic bulletins which are mailed to all regular customers. The types of music specialized in are blues, R&B, rockabilly, folk, country, old-timey, bluegrass, vintage jazz and ethnic music from many areas. The company is owned by Chris Strachwitz and Frank Scott — they keep in touch with most musical events in the fields listed above and will gladly give callers information.

Arhoolie Records, a label operated by Chris Strachwitz specializing in American regional folk music and ethnic musics like blues, Cajun, country and Tex-Mex.

Back Room Distribution Co. Owned by Arhoolie and run by Chris, Frank and a few other helpers, Back Room distributes many fine labels to record shops, not just in Northern California but all over the world. It carries Rounder, Folkways, Philo, Yazoo, Delmark, County, Goldband, Swallow, Rebel and many other US folk and regional labels, as well as imports like Sonet from the UK and Sweden and Swaggie from Australia. Record shops should send $2 for a complete catalogue.

Flower Films Co. Upstairs in the same building, film maker Les Blank can sometimes be found editing his latest documentary on some form of American regional music. Notable Les Blank films include "Chulas Fronteras," already mentioned in the Tex-Mex chapter; "Always For Pleasure," a joyous look at pre-Mardi Gras festivities and the Jazz Heritage Festival in New Orleans; "Hot Pepper," about zyedco musician Clifton Cheiner; "Spend It All," about Cajun music and featuring The Balfa Brothers; "The Blues According To Lightnin' Hopkins," about the great Houston-based bluesman; and "A Well Spent Life," featuring another Texan, Mance Lipscomb.

Write to Flower Films at the above address for details of buying or hiring these films.

Beserkley Records, "The Home of the Hits." One of the first of the backroom labels of the seventies, Beserkley was formed by ex-law student Matthew Kaufman in his home area of Berkeley. The first single released was by Earth Quake, a local group managed by

Kaufman who were dissatisfied with working for a huge corporation. Matthew went on to discover Jonathan Richman and the Modern Lovers singing in a California bar. When a record they made for Warner Brothers was shelved, Beserkley bought the tapes and released the album. It became a sought after import in England and established Beserkley as a "cult" label. At the time of writing, Beserkley is better distributed in England than in the US, but all this is expected to change and before long acts like Greg Kihn, The Rubinoos and The Modern Lovers are expected to be household names.

NORTH BAY CLUBS

The Inn of the Beginning, downtown Cotati, (707) 795-9955. Excellent club with a relaxed atmosphere and a varied selection of quality folk, country and blues-based music. Between sets, music from KVRE 101.7 FM out of Santa Rosa, one of the best radio stations in Northern California.

Gatsby's, 39 Caledonia, Sausalito, 332-4500. Jazz and occasional blues.

Old Mill Tavern, 106 Throckmorton, Mill Valley, 388-9927. Country/rock, folk and blues. While in Mill Valley, check out the local record shop Village Music for a comprehensive collection of country, folk and ethnic music plus lots of bargains for as little as $1.

Sweetwater, 153 Throckmorton, Mill Valley. Jazz and rock acts.

The Laguna, 234 S. Main, Sebastapol, (707) 823-5240. Rock, folk and country.

SOUTH BAY CLUBS

Eulipa Cafe, 372 S. 1st St., San Jose, 293-6818. Excellent musical fare of top flight jazz and blues names.

Laundry Works, 87 N. San Pedro, San Jose, 287-1456. Local rock talent.

Chuck's Cellar, 4926 El Camino Real, Los Altos, 964-0220. Name and local folk, country, rock and jazz acts featured.

Mainliner Club, 4031 Pacific Blvd., San Mateo. Occasional zydeco dances here.

Bodega, 30 S. Central, Campbell, (408) 374-4000. Local rock place.

(Special thanks for their help with the San Francisco area to *John Platt, Mike Bailey, Gary* and *Cynthia Blake.)*

TEXAS

Those of you who are keen to hear the earthier, funkier kinds of music, and in relatively informal surroundings, should be well satisfied with Texas, a state whose music draws heavily on a range of traditional styles that came out of the South — blues, rhythm and blues, traditional country, rockabilly, rock 'n' roll and western swing. A surprising amount of localized ethnic music forms have survived here and can still be found, including Cajun, Tex-Mex and Czech polka.

The popular misconception about Texas as a vast area containing nothing but oil, cattle, dust, hungry rattlesnakes and greedy, vulgar people, needs to be laid to rest. Texans are among the friendliest people in the country and their state offers an amazing array of contrasts — the scenery changes from pine forests in the east to treeless plains of prairie grass in the west to palm trees and orange groves along the valley of the Rio Grande, the mighty river that is the country's border with Mexico. The climate is pleasant and there is plenty of sunshine all year round.

Houston

Houston is a city for winners, not losers — "the capital of the fast buck." It's the fastest growing American city thanks to oil, its location on the pleasant "sun belt," its low taxes and the cheap cost of living. For the poor it can be close to hell, social spending is about the lowest in the US, and the police are among the most brutal.

Though the atmosphere is sometimes comfortable, the music here is frequently amazing, especially on the small club level. Many of the most influential musicians in blues, rock and country come from around here, and the city remains an important breeding ground for talented musicians. The local blues and zydeco scenes are strong but you'd be unwise to try and seek them out unless you can get help from locals who know the clubs.

Come to Houston with friends in a car or try to arrange to stay with someone, as this is not a good place to be on your own — public transport is poor and cab fares to some of the best clubs are prohibitive. Not far from downtown Houston is the Montrose area centered on Montrose Boulevard and not unlike Greenwich Village in New York or the French Quarter in New Orleans with its several small cafes and bars. Here you are likely to meet friendly, helpful people and find cheap music places.

Check the "Nightlife Section" of the *Houston Chronicle* for what's on, the Saturday section being especially useful for the week ahead. The *Houston City Magazine* has a useful section that will guide you to the best local clubs and discos.

CONCERTS

Astrodome, 748-4500. Six miles out of town is the world's first air-conditioned sports stadium covered by an unsupported dome and worth a visit in its own right. It features occasional rock concerts by (very) big names.

Miller Outdoor Theater, Hermann Park, 222-3576. In the summer there are several impressive music events here — all free — including the Houston Folk Festival and the Juneteenth Blues Festival (highly recommended) held here each June on the anniversary of the liberation of the slaves in Texas.

CLUBS

Gilley's, 4500 Spencer Hwy., Pasadena, 941-7990. The personification of Texas redneck popular culture, this is one of the biggest honky tonks in the world, large enough to herd cattle through. Owned by country singer Mickey Gilley, the club features a nightly bill of Texas country music and some of the best dancing (from customers) that you'll see anywhere. The mechanical bucking bull is recommended for only the most foolhardy. Saturday night at Gilley's is an absolute must, but you'll need your own transport.

Whiskey River, 8670 S. Gessner, 777-5225. Local bands during the week including the talented Vince Vance and the Valiants, and nationally known names on weekends.

Fool's Gold, 5901 Westheimer at Fountain View, 780-0750. Cowboy disco and singles bar. According to *Houston City Magazine* you'll know you're there by the number of pickup trucks with gun racks in the parking lot!

Anderson Fair, 2007 Grant, 528-8576. Houston's premier folk club and the hub of the Montrose music circuit. If you want to hear Lightnin' Hopkins — still living and working in this area — someone here should be able to tell you where to find him playing. Local country/folk talent including Tex Bell and Mickey White (the infamous Hemmer Ridge Mountain Boys), Richard Dobson, Don Saunders and the highly unbelievable Frank Davis (all recommended.)

Houlihan's No. 2, 128 Westheimer, 528-1835. Another popular Montrose area folk club. Writer's night Monday.

Fitzgerald's, 2706 White Oak, 862-7580. Great old two-story building in Houston Heights. Live music on two floors — jazz, blues and folk.

Club Laveek, 1511 Blodgett, 528-8267. Black club featuring name jazz talent.

Cody's, 3400 Montrose, 522-9747. Classy jazz place on the ninth floor which offers a spectacular view of the city at night.

La Provence, 3215 Main, 528-5577. Comfortable jazz cafe with the best local talent. The Sunday afternoon jam sessions are recommended.

Paradise Island, 4705 Main, 528-8394. New wave rock.

(Special thanks to *John Lomax*).

Dallas/Fort Worth

Dallas and Fort Worth lie only about 31 miles apart, share the biggest airport in the world, but are remarkably different in character. Dallas is the financial and cultural center of Texas — big, brash and bold; while Fort Worth is still very western — it began as a watering hole for cowboys and their longhorn steer on the Chisholm trail and continues as the headquarters for the cattle industry. Much of the Old West has been preserved around the historic stockyards area north of the town.

Musically neither town has as much to offer on a local level as Houston, but there should be enough to satisfy most taste buds over a short visit. The bi-monthly free magazine *Buddy* will guide you to the good gigs while the Friday morning edition of the *Dallas Morning News* has a comprehensive guide to the week ahead.

DALLAS CONCERT HALLS

The really big concerts — Bob Dylan, Billy Joel — are at the Dallas Convention Center. Most other major acts play The Palladium on Northwest Highway, a comfortable and intimate theater.

DALLAS CLUBS

Longhorn Ballroom, 216 Corinth, 428-3128. A wonderful old Texas country ballroom. Al Harvey and the Longhorn Band play Western swing Wed. to Sat. Monday night is blues with big names like Bobby Bland.

The Binary Star, 3121 Inwood Rd., 351-9019. Popular modern rock club with local bands. According to *Buddy*, "18-25 young freak crowd — great place to pick up men and women."

Sneaky Pete's Rock 'n' Roll Heaven, 714 Medallion Center, Skillman at NW Hwy., 369-1874. One of the better listening clubs in the Dallas area — local rock bands.

Strictly Tabu, 4111 Lomo Alto, 526-9325. Dallas' bastion of traditional jazz. Several clubs in Dallas feature jazz — the free newspaper *Texas Jazz*, available from record shops, will guide you to the best places.

Czech Club, 4930 Military Pkwy., 321-3135. Czech polka music from Bill Kucera and the Czechmates.

Grapevine Opry, Grapevine. A few miles north of Fort Worth/Dallas you'll find the home of the Grapevine Opry on Main Street. Chisai Childs bought the old Palace Theater which here and now showcases local country talent each Saturday. Manager Johnnie High explains — "One word we never use is amateur. Everybody is treated with respect here and the place is kept clean. There's no drinking and no smoking allowed inside. People here know they can bring their grandmother, their mother and their kids without hearing someone sing "I'm the Only Hell My Mother Ever Raised."

RECORD AND BOOK SHOPS

Stacks O'Tracks, 2817 Greenville, Ave., No. 6, 823-4261. Used/collector record store run by Curtis Hawkins has masses of fascinating musical memorabilia for sale — promotional buttons, T-shirts, posters, photos.

Half Price Books, Records and Magazines, 4535 McKinney Ave. Main store of an unusual Texan chain that has huge stocks of second-hand records and magazines. Items dating from 1581 to last month's *Texas Monthly*. Other stores can be found by checking the phone books in Austin, Waco, Temple and San Antonio.

(Special thanks to *Stoney Burns*)

FORT WORTH CLUBS

Fast Eddie's, 4400 White Settlement Rd., 735-1199. Local rock and blues bands Wed. through Sat.

Stargazer Rock and Roll, 2800 Azie Ave., 626-0911. Large rock 'n' roll showcase.

New Bluebird Niteclub, Horne and Wellesley, 737-0453. An absolute must for R&B fans. An authentic Texas R&B joint that rocks every weekend evening with the music of Robert Ealey and his Five Careless Lovers. Ealey's band seems to be different every time you visit, but it usually contains some members of the Juke Jumpers, an excellent band in their own right who perform a mix of blues, rockabilly and jazz.

Tack's Fun House, 1101 E. 11th off Interstate 35, east of downtown, 335-0476. Friday and Saturday nights U.P. Wilson is featured. U.P. is a remarkable blues musician. Though crippled, he somehow manages to play with one hand.

White Elephant Saloon, 106 E. Exchange, 624-1887. Open every night except Sunday — country music performed in a club with frontier-style decor. Located in the Cowtown area which is like the set of a cowboy movie. There's a rodeo in this area each year in late September with lots of music.

RECORD SHOPS

Sybil's Golden Oldies, 5417 E. Lancaster. Good for gospel and Mexican music but can be expensive.

Record Town, 3025 University Drive, 926-1331. Good for blues, rock 'n' roll and jazz. Run by Sumter Bruton who moonlights in the Juke Jumpers and can help you locate good music from Fort Worth's finest including Delbert McClinton.

Taylor's Record Collections Warehouse, 543-8781. John Taylor has a large warehouse and three houses full of records — he deals in all kinds of music though fans of blues, R&B and country should be particularly pleased with what they might find. Phone for an appointment.

(Thanks to *Christina Patoski, Jim Yanaway* and *Ted Tucker*)

Austin

Many people think of Austin, the Texas capital, as the center of outlaw country music and although Willie Nelson and Jerry Jeff Walker have homes here it's a reputation that's now out of date. Austin is a hotbed of live music of all kinds — Latin, jazz, new wave rock, Tex-Mex, blues, Americanized reggae, traditional country, bluegrass and rockabilly.

Several big names play the town but the best music is to be found in the dozens of small clubs that hold from 100 to 600 and charge a couple of dollars admission. Good music is cheap and plentiful and a visit is highly recommended.

AUSTIN CONCERT HALLS

Big names play at the new University Special Events Center — SEC, Super Drum — which is expensive but has surprisingly good sound. Manor Downs is a good open air place on the site of the old quarter horse race track to the east of town.

The Armadillo at 525 Barton Springs and the Austin Opry House at 200 Academy are atmospheric music emporiums and ideal places to hear the biggest local names as well as national acts.

AUSTIN CLUBS

Soap Creek Saloon, 11306 N. Lamar. Austin's best known club now located in an old country and western ballroom where Bob Wills and Hank Williams were once regulars. A good place to see local favorites like Alvin Crow (Western swing), Marcia Ball (goodtime R&B and modern country), Ray Campi (rockabilly), Delbert McClinton (a talented white R&B dinger from Fort Worth) and the club's house band, the Uranium Savages (who are crazy).

Silver Dollar, 9233 Burnet Rd., 837-1824. Enormous dance hall for hard core country. A great place to see perfectly executed examples of Texan dances like the Cotton Eyed Joe and the Texas Two Step.

Broken Spoke, 2301 S. Lamar, 442-6189. One of Austin's oldest hard core country dance places. Rustic place — wear your cowboy boots and hat.

Raul's, 2610 Guadalupe, 477-1431. One time Chicano showcase and now premier new wave rock spot.

Rome Inn, 29th and Rio Grande, 476-6111. Blues center since the closure of the excellent Antones. Features local white blues revivalists like the Fabulous Thunderbirds who are excellent.

HONKY TONKIN'

The Back Room, 2201 E. Riverside, 441-4677. This little club has spawned some of the finest bands to come out of Austin. "It's a pickers hangout and there are occasional impromptu jam sessions."

Casablanca, 304 W. 15th St., 472-7355. This is "Rick's American Bar" after the Bogart movie. Classy place with palms, wicker seats and good jazz.

RECORDS AND BOOK SHOPS

OK Records and Books, 137 E. 6th St. Thousands of new and used blues/R&B records.

Madonado Record Shop, 1114 E. 1st St. Mexican record store.

Half Price Records and Books. Two stores at 1514 Lavaca and 6103 Burnet Rd.

RECORD LABEL

B.F. Deal, 608-B W. North Loop, Austin, Texas 78751. Owned by singer/songwriter Mike Williams, an amusing local character and author of such gems as "I'm Playing the Jukebox to Remember What I'm Drinking To Forget" and "I'm From Dumb Ass Texas." The B.F. Deal Sampler (B.F. Deal 5) and "Smilin" by Bill and Bonnie Herne (B.F. Deal 7) are recommended. Bill and Bonnie are a blind couple who've been singing their pure, honest and hard-working brand of country music in the clubs and bars of Texas for over 10 years.

(Thanks to *Steve Sagik* and *Joe Nick Patoski*)

San Antonio

Possibly the most pleasant city in Texas. The Alamo is in the middle and the most important tourist attraction. There's a large Spanish population supporting three radio stations and hundreds of icehouses, dancehalls and bars concentrated on the West and Southside. Icehouses are San Antonio's version of the convenience store. They have a long-standing reputation as a primary social gathering spot. Before the era of air-conditioning, icehouses were the only neighborhood spots where people could cool off and drink beer in the summer. Today most San Antonio icehouses still contain an area for beer drinking, conversation and music.

Lovers of the macabre should check out the local San Antonio television when it's running the local news. Nowhere in America will you see such a succession of blood, gore and grief-stricken people. Camera teams seem to arrive at accidents while the wheels are still spinning! *Action* is a monthly paper published out of the city that calls itself "The Texas Entertainment Magazine" and has interesting articles on the local scene and carries advertisements for some of the clubs.

SAN ANTONIO CLUBS

The Bijou, 4106 San Pedro, 732-3664. Easy-going, comfortable atmosphere at this saloon which features a variety of music including jazz (on Thursdays), country and rock.

The Alamo Fish Market and Bakery, 159 Commerce. Modern jazz on weekends.

The Landing, Riverwalk Sq., 223-7266. Local jazz favorites the Happy Jazz Band play here most nights.

LOCAL RECORD LABEL

Texas Re-Cord, Box 19, Bulvarde, Texas 78163. One man doing all he can for the music of San Antonio is Augie Meyers (one-time organist with the Sir Douglas Quintet). He now has his own group, the Western Head Band, which plays around the Southwest, an occasional radio show on KMAC and his own record label which promotes the best of the area's music. His sound is a blend of Mexican, Black and Anglo cultures. Other acts include "Wild Ray" Liberto, Publio Casillas and Doug Sahm.

Luckenbach

It could be difficult finding Luckenbach, a minute town in the hills near Fredericksburg, because souvenir hunters have ripped off every sign with the name on it. Luckenbach was founded in 1849 and bought by Hondo Crouch in 1971. Crouch, a white-bearded, angelic-looking man and possibly the most befriended man in Texas, put on a series of zany productions including "The Mad Dauber Festival" and "The Luckenbach World Fair." Jerry Jeff Walker recorded his "Viva Terlingua" album here in 1973 and Waylon Jennings had a huge crossover hit with "Luckenbach — Back to the Basics of Life." The town has now become a big tourist attraction with people who take the song seriously — they drive into Fredericksburg in huge trailers, get a horse out of the back and spend the weekend riding around the area. Hondo Crouch died of a heart attack in 1976, leaving the town with a population of three humans, a flock of chickens and an alcoholic pig called Mona Lisa. There are only about four buildings but one is a dance hall. Every Saturday there's a dance — booze has to be bought from across the street from the ice-filled troughs outside the post office. The Mud Daubers Fair is still held here each year, but the World's Fair has moved to Fredericksburg due to the lack of sanitary facilities — Luckenbach is still just a two-hole town.

Lubbock

Lubbock, a piece of bland suburbia stuck in the middle of all the cotton fields you can imagine in the West Texas plains. It's as flat as a pancake and has a wind that blows night and day; a wind that is seen as an important inspiration to the many musicians who've come from these parts and the driving force that makes them all want to leave town. Lubbock's most famous son is Buddy Holly but others associated with these parts include Waylon Jennings, country comedian Dan Bowman (both DJs here in the fifties), Roy

Orbison, Mac Davis, Jimmy Gilmer and The Fireballs, Sonny Curtis and Joe Ely.

Five miles out of town lies the Cotton Club where young Lubbock comes to dance on a Saturday night. Otherwise there's little in the way of musical action. Most musical tourists come to see Buddy Holly's grave (he died in an air crash in 1959). He's buried in the City of Lubbock Cemetery on the east side of town at the end of 34th Street. Until the release of the movie "The Buddy Holly Story," the singer went without much recognition in his hometown; but there's going to be an annual concert each September on the anniversary of his birthday.

TEX-MEX AND THE REGIONAL MUSIC OF TEXAS

Texas is rich in music of many kinds, particularly rock, blues and country. It's also produced some unique musical styles and variants that are little known and seldom heard outside the Southwest. Many are ethnic music hybrids that have somehow survived almost intact through many decades and have resisted the homogenizing processes of the mass media.

The Lone Star State is home to a large number of ethnic groups and the descendants of Africans, Germans, Czechs, Poles, French, Mexicans and many others can be found in their own distinct areas and city neighborhoods. In this enormous state individuality has always been encouraged, and many groups have deliberately resisted cultural dilution while others have been rurally or socially isolated, which explains why cultural traditions have been retained and nurtured.

Today, if you can penetrate the various communities, you'll find in roadhouses, honky tonks and dancehalls Czech polka bands, Cajun and zydeco groups, German oom-pah bands, Greek bouzouki bands and conjunto outfits, all playing their own Texas-influenced brands of music.

Here, with the considerable help of Texas-based journalist Joe Nick Patoski and the English musicologist Tony Russell, is a brief introduction to a few of the interesting music scenes that can be found — with a bit of effort and searching around — in the Texas backwaters.

Tex-Mex

Heading west for San Antonio from Houston or south from Austin you'll have no trouble finding Mexican radio stations playing pop music sung in Spanish. This is Tejano country where you'll find Mexicans of Texan descent. The records on the radio, from the likes of Wally Gonzales, are lively and interesting — certainly more so than the mellow pop on the top-40 stations — but it's quite a long way from the traditional Tex-Mex music that's played by people like Flaco Jiminez. Flaco and his small band comprising accordian, bajo-sexto and rhythm guitar collaborated with Ry Cooder on an American and European tour a few years ago. Their music isn't always easy to discover as Tony Russell reports:

"There are musicians with followings like Flaco and his rival Mongo Saldivar, but most conjunto is a scuffling business conducted in small clubs for the not exactly young. Like blues in Chicago, in fact, though without the patronage of a white campus population.

"In the dancehalls you will more probably find bands with featured singers, and brass sections rather than accordians, and sometimes even synthesizers. These groups can be unbelievably loud. If you want a drink within 200 yards of them you either write it down or wait for an intermission.

"Tex-Mex is a fashionable term but an outsider's, I think, and not necessarily OK on the spot. The community as a whole prefers to be called Spanish-American. Whatever it's called, this music is in some respects at the point where urban Black music was at 15 or 20 years ago, when the old fashioned blues and R&B musicians were being eased out to the smaller and less glamorous places, to be succeeded by a generation with a lot of flash and a new repertoire. Like then, the new Mexican music in Texas is backed by a powerful radio and record industry.

"You can't, therefore, be all that optimistic about the future of conjunto music. But it hangs on after a fashion, well enough, and its roots are evident even in hit records."

Joe Nick Patoski introduces some of the best known musicians:
Flaco Jiminez — "In San Antonio, only one musician gets away with calling himself 'El Ray de Texas' (The King) — Flaco. His father, Santiago, the original 'El Flaco' (The Skinny One), dominated the pack in South Texas for over 30 years before he retired and handed his crown over to his son. Young Flaco wears it well. Without resorting to gimmicks or too many Freddy Fender songs, he is currently the prime exporter of authentic Tejano music to the gringos. He's played cameos on major albums by Doug Sahm and Ry Cooder. After his tour with Cooder he was soon back making his Texas dancehall circuit, driving 300 miles from Lubbock in one afternoon to make the big Sunday dance at the Rockin' M east of Austin. Outside big Chicano cities like San Antonio and Corpus Christi, Sundays are the customary dance nights because that is the only night most country music dancehalls allow Tejanos to have

their show. Hee, on familiar turf, he is the same old Flaco Jr., where his conjunto is not an artifact to be examined by anthropologists but a dance machine that cooks with polkas, boleros, rancheros from northern Mexico, waltzes and even an occasional rump-rolling cumbia to please the trendy teens."

Steve Jordon — "His five-piece conjunto, Rio Jordon, tours the piscas (migrant) circuit in a battered yellow school bus, playing dances for migrant Chicano farmworkers from Florida to Washington. He's a leading innovator in the Chicano underground, he's the musicians' musician, capable of playing 35 different instruments. He's a genius of the accordian and the prime candidate for stardom in the event rock 'n' roll should admit Tex-Mex influences again.

"Jordon's current dance mix is liberally sprinkled with enough polkas to satisfy the old guard while including enough experimentation to dazzle the brown boppers. He has the fastest and most versatile finger work of all the Texas squeeze-box artists, coaxing jazz and bebop licks out of the same crude diatonic button accordian that every lead player uses. He's seen the world, too, playing in the bands of recognized jazzmen like Jimmy Smith, Jack McDuff and Willie Bobo. After a lengthy stint in the big-time music hustle, he returned to his native South Texas soil, where he begun playing professionally at the age of seven."

Los Alegres de Teran — "A very small ethnic band comprising just two men: Eugene Abrego on accordian and Tomas Ortiz on bajo-sexto. They've been together for over 25 years and have made over 40 albums. They are known for carefully harmonized vocals, simple accompaniment and their repertoire of ballads that tell stories of courage and romance. They're based in McAllen, Texas."

Jose Morantes — "For a living Jose runs the El Norteno record distributorship in the rear of his well-kept white frame house at 2606 Ruis, San Antonio, but for pleasure he interprets the news in self-penned corridos. Descended from the twelfth century Spanish romantic epic, corridos have flourished in South Texas since the first Mexicans settled in the area. The songs enjoyed their strongest support between the 1830s and the 1930s when they faded away with the advent of the mass media. Although corridos have been written on any subject worth discussing in the community, the classic repeats one basic story — somewhere along the border, a lone Mexican defends his honor in the face of cowardly rinches, the Texas Rangers, who symbolize all Anglos of dubious intent. Morantes has been writing for over 35 years and is the dean of San

Antonio corridodistas."

WHERE TO HEAR TEX-MEX MUSIC

Rockin' M Club, State Hwy. 183 between Lockhart and Austin. They have a big dance here each Sunday; show up by 5PM to be sure of a seat. The big attraction is Flaco Jiminez, though others appear. Accordian battle dances have been very popular recently. The dance lasts until midnight and is sometimes broadcast over KNXX in Austin. Joe Nick Patoski describes a visit: "A public dance that is a full-grown party. Bottles are piled up on the paper-covered tables, along with containers of food and picnic baskets. A flaming-hot cheese sauce, chile con queso, is freely offered to strangers, a test to discover if they are turistas or just folks. If the dance floor is any indication, no generation gap exists among conjunto aficionados. The sawdust-covered wooden floor is packed with dancers of all ages, gliding in a counterclockwise flow like roller skaters."

La Plaza, 6th St., Austin. Nightly conjunto music.

La Fuente Super Ballroom on Zarzamora, San Antonio.

Alma Latina Dinner Club on Zarzamora, San Antonio. A mile south from La Fuente.

Mendiola's Ballroom, S. Hwy. 81, near San Antonio. Look out for appearances by Los Pavos Reales here.

La Villita, Old Kingsville Rd., at the edge of Alice.

La Villa Real, Hwy. 83 near McAllen. Tuesday night is conjunto night.

Alma Latina, Rainbow Shopping Center, Dickinson.

An excellent film has been made about the music and culture of the conjuntos in Texas. "Chulas Fronteras" directed by Les Blank, conceived and directed by Chris Strachwitz, can be bought or hired from Brazos Films, 10341 San Pablo Avenue, El Cerrito, California. Flaco Jiminez and the unique Los Alegres de Teran are among the musicians featured in the film and on the excellent soundtrack album, which is available on Chris Strachwitz' Arhoolie record label from the same address.

Tex-Mex glossary of terms: Tejano — any Chicano born and raised in Texas. **Accordion** — the electric guitar of Tejano music. These accordions are stripped down and simpler than the familiar piano-key models. **Bajo-sexto** — a 12-string guitar with open tuning, constructed in Mexico or South Texas. Strummed, not picked, bajos are the rhythm backbone of a conjunto. **Conjunto** — a band of fewer than six pieces, usually led by an accordion. **Orquestas** — large bands in which the organ is replaced by organ and horn sections. The music is usually much slicker, more uptown than that of the conjuntos. **Jalapeno** — a fiery hot pepper known to bring tears and perspiration to the uninitiated eater.

Czech and German Polka Music

Draw a triangle in southeastern Texas, with the San Antonio-Houston highway as the base and Waco as its apex, and you have an area that contains many German, Bohemian and Czech communities. Weekend dances feature the music of polka bands like the Red Ravens, the Fritz Hodde Band and many more. Their music is loud, exuberant and dominated by crisp horn sections. Lee Roy Matocha leads a band and also broadcasts polka music on the radio. He calls himself, with some justification, "King of the Nation's Polka Shows" and broadcasts 25 programs on 10 different stations within this area. Modern polka bands use electric bass, and sometimes lead guitar where the old style had the horns doing nearly all the work — one of Lee Roy's programs is all polka oldies when he makes sure that the traditional music isn't forgotten. (*Tony Russell*).

The Baca Band, led by Gil Baca, is the oldest and most famous of the Czech bands. Formed in 1892 by Gil's grandfather, they've been playing polka music in and around their home town of Fayetteville ever since. The band's oldest member, Ray Baca Sr., has a 120-string dulcimer which he plays with mallets. The Baca Band are probably the easiest of the Texas-based Czech polka bands to be found as they often play at big festivals like the annual Texas Folklife event in San Antonio.

Cajun and Zydeco

The good-time French music from across the border in Louisiana, described in a previous chapter, overflows into parts of East Texas. The last Saturday in the month is a big night in Beaumont for zydeco fans as that's the night of the big "la-la" dance at Our Mother of Mercy Catholic Church Hall. Ten miles southwest of Beaumont is Cheek (on highway 124) and the Ten Acre Club here is a regular stopping point on the zydeco circuit for groups like Marcel Dugas and the Entertainers and Good Rocking Dopsie and the Cajun Twisters. Close to the Texas/Louisiana border is Bridge City, where you'll probably still be able to find a club called Sparkle Paradise at 108 Texas Avenue. Zydeco star Clifton Chenier plays here from time to time.

Allen Thidbodeaux and his French Ramblers play traditional Cajun music and are based in Groves, Texas, though came originally from Sulphur, Louisiana. Their regular Sunday night gig is at the Rodair Club on Highway 365 in Port Arthur.

Texas Fiddle Music

The stranger thinks of oil wells, the native of chicken fried steaks and Lone Star beer. But for music, the emblem of Texas must be the fiddle. The first country music ever recorded was by a Texas fiddler called Eck Robertson and "Texas Style" dominates Southern fiddling contests today. Western swing, Texas' most influential contribution to country music, is essentially fiddle music.

Any summer weekend you can find fiddle contests in Texas. There are several big events but also plenty of little contests, held in school houses and church halls. Keep your eyes open for placards advertising upcoming events. You can play safe and wait for a big-time event like a "Grand Masters" contest, but these can be wearisome affairs with all the excitement organized out of them. Away from the big league, however, where the prize money isn't so lavish as to scare the spirit out of a musician, you can hear all the idiosyncrasies of local tunes. The M.C. works from a scrap of schoolbook paper, and the fiddlers work from the heart. And not just from the stage: your three or four minutes at the microphone (one breakdown, one waltz, one selection of own choice) make a formal purpose for your trip, but the hours outside the hall, picking and picnicking in the sun, are why you have come. (*Tony Russell*)

Western Swing

Western swing was a brand of music that enjoyed enormous popularity in the Southwest, most notably in Texas and Oklahoma, in the late thirties and forties. Bob Wills and his Texas Playboys were the best known and most popular and are still remembered today for their regular radio broadcasts and Saturday night dances. The music that Wills and his band played was a glorious mixture of big band swing, country, blues, jazz and gospel.

By the start of the fifties the music had begun to lose favor and the arrival of Elvis Presley and rock 'n' roll in the mid-fifties were to sound the death knoll. Few musicians found it economically worthwhile to continue playing in the old style and either traded their steel guitars and fiddles for electric guitars or retired. Little more was heard of Western swing until the early seventies, when there was a revival of interest in the music — Bob Wills albums were re-issued, surviving members of his old band began playing concerts and making records again, and young musicians began recreating the sound. The best young Western swing band around today is Alvin Crow and his Pleasant Valley Boys who are based in Austin, Texas.

One Western swing band never gave up in the face of rock 'n' roll. They're Hoyle Nix and his Cowboy Band, who've been playing together since 1946. They're a household word in the 250-mile radius of their tiny home town of Big Spring, where they've been performing every Saturday night for over 30 years at Hoyle Nix's Stampede Club, but little known elsewhere in Texas, let alone outside the state.

Turkey is a very small town in the Texas panhandle — if you went west from Tulsa you'd probably run into it — which is very proud to be "the home of Bob Wills." There's a Bob Wills Monument (he died in 1975) and a museum that's open every afternoon. The best day to visit is on the last Saturday of April — Bob Wills Celebration Day — when there is a parade with every sort of float imaginable that could have something to do with Bob Wills. There's a fiddler's contest and a Western swing concert featuring original members of Bob's band.

Hearing the Regional Music of Texas

Most music in Texas is best heard on a Saturday night in the local honky tonk or roadhouse where people get down to the simple pleasures of dancing, drinking and generally having a good time with their own favorite brand of music. This isn't always easy to locate or enter into, so an alternative that could well enable you to experience several kinds of music is to visit one of the many festivals. Here is a selection:

Texas State Championship Fiddler's Frolics, K.C. Hall and Fairgrounds, Hwy. 77S, Hallettsville. Weekend in late April. Info: (512) 798-3608.

Polka Festival, Ennis. Polka bands, Czech food and beer. Weekend in early May.

Kerrville Folk Festival, Quiet Valley Ranch, Kerrville. Call organizer Rod Kennedy (512) 896-3800 for details of his various annual festivals held here. The folk festival, featuring a variety of Texas and ethnic musics, is held each May.

Harry C. Smith Old Time Fiddler's Contest held at Harry's home near Paris. Call (214) 785-1000 for information of this festival usually held in July.

Texas Folklife Festival, Institute of Texan Cultures, downtown San Antonio on Hemis Fair Plaza. Held over three or four days in early August. Write to P.O. Box 1226, San Antonio, Texas 78294 for details of this year's events.

Wurstfest, New Braunfels. Weeklong salute to the area's sausage industry which is highlighted by food, beer and polka music. Early November.

TULSA, OKLAHOMA

The Tulsa music tradition is rich with rock 'n' roll, rhythm and blues, country music and Western swing. It was Bob Wills, the "King of Western Swing" who put the town on the musical map when he began his famous radio broadcasts over KVOO and live shows from the famous Cain's ballroom in 1934. Several well-known musicians were brought up in Tulsa, including J.J. Cale (Johnny then), David Gates, Leon Russell (Russell Bridges then) and Elvin Bishop who were all at Will Rogers High School together in the fifties.

Today Tulsa is a booming oil and cattle town, set amidst the green rolling hills of the Creek, Osage and Cherokee nations. The city is increasingly developing into a world force in terms of country music, thanks to the efforts of the Jim Halsey Co., Inc. which is based here. The Tulsa International Music Festival is organized each Fall. It's a unique event that began as an annual ranch party given by Halsey as a "thank you" to the talent bookers, music industry and media for supporting his acts. There are still activities for the music business people but several concerts and shows are open to the general public.

CLUBS

Cain's Ballroom, 423 N. Main St., 582-2078 or 584-2309. There can't be many clubs in America that can claim to have featured both Hank Williams and the Sex Pistols in their respective heydays. Cain's can, and a lot more besides. This ballroom has a musical heritage as rich as the city's and many young Tulsans can remember their parents talking of the days when Bob Wills and his Texas Playboys performed while bootleg whisky was sold out in the back from an old Chevy pick-up. Owner Larry Shaeffer, who's probably Oklahoma's most successful promoter, books big name country, rock and jazz talent. There is an excellent bar, a large dance floor and the walls are covered with pictures and posters of Bob Wills, Tex Williams and other famous country music names. The hall has been nominated for designation as a national historic site so will hopefully be around for many more years to come. Don't miss the chance of a visit.

Mickey's Country Darlin's, 2802 S. Harvard, 742-9159. Country rock nightspot and home for Mickey Crocker and his Oklahoma Thunder Band. Mickey hosts local and national acts.

Caravan Ballroom, 7901 E. 41st St., 663-5468. There's usually a dance here on Saturday nights with the Caravan Band. Johnnie Lee Wills plays here occasionally — Johnnie Lee is Bob Wills' brother and lives in Tulsa where he owns a Western Store which he runs with his son John Thomas.

Cedar Creek Saloon, 1108 S. Lewis, 932-9157. For bluegrass and progressive country music, Cedar Creek is hard to beat. The emphasis is on local talent, but they do bring in out-of-town people. Some of the talented locals you're likely to find here include Randy Crouch and Flying Horse, The Blueweed Boys and the Nairobi Trio.

Stefano's, 11103 E. 31st St., 663-6278. The emphasis is again local. Live music Wednesday through Saturday nights. Thursday is amateur night.

J. Michael's Stage Door, 1164 S. Garnett Rd., 437-9772. Restaurant and club that occasionally books national country acts.

Paradise Club, 6216 S. Lewis, 742-9368. Good spot for jazz, blues and country name talent.

(Special thanks to *Ellis Widner*)

WASHINGTON, DC

The nation's capital and the focus for political activity, Washington isn't famous as a musical center but offers a pleasing range of good music on a local level from jazz to rock and just about everything except middle-of-the-road pop. Washington is acknowledged as the bluegrass capital of the country and some of the best bands play here regularly (bluegrass clubs and bands are listed in the next chapter).

The city provides a good base for anyone traveling with people who aren't great music fans — there's a lots to see and do, several excellent museums, theaters including the infamous Ford Theater where Abraham Lincoln was assassinated and which still has live stage shows, and world famous buildings and monuments. Washington is only a couple of hours' drive from ocean and coastal resorts like Chesapeake Bay, the misty blue Appalachian mountains or historic Virginia.

The capital has a cruciform shape and is divided into four geographical sections centering on the political area that includes the White House. The major tourist attractions and many of the clubs are located in the NW area. Visitors without their own transport are advised to base themselves near the fashionable Georgetown section where there's more than enough musical action available, including three of Washington's best clubs, the Cellar Door, Desperado's and Blues Alley. Cab rates to some of the other good clubs, located in the suburbs, are likely to be prohibitive.

Washington has produced many excellent musicians including Roy Buchanan, The Clovers, Jim Morrison, Emmylou Harris, Donald Byrd, Link Wray, Gil Scott-Heron, Clyde McPhatter, Lloyd Price, Pete Seeger, Billy Stewart, Don Covay, John Fahey, Roy Clark and Duke Ellington. But, as local writer and musician William Holland explains, "Washington has always been a seedbed for national talent, but with the exception of a very few hometowners, most have had to leave D.C. to achieve any national recognition. However, Roberta Flack was discovered here at the old Mr. Henry's by Les McCann, Nils Lofgren showed up at the Cellar Door one night and played his way into Neil Young's heart, and Ruth Brown was discovered singing in a local club by Cab

Calloway's wife."

The standard of musicianship of many of the area's bands is surprisingly high. Local clubs have always made a point of supporting home-based groups, and there's considerable encouragement from the monthly paper *The Unicorn Times* and local radio. A number of long established bands and musicians deserve special mention. The Seldom Scene, featuring dobro player Mike Auldridge, is probably the best bluegrass band in the country (see next chapter) while The Nighthawks are often hailed as the best white blues band in the US. The gritty Chicago blues-inspired rock served up by this Washington-based four-piece has been exciting club-goers in this area for years and famous musicians seek the band out when they're in town. Danny Gatton is D.C.'s quasi-legendary guitarists' guitarist who's come out of a long tradition of Southern stylists like Scotty Moore and James Burton and his local predecessors like Link Wray and Roy Buchanan. His problem is not how to play but what to play and who with. Payday (formerly The Rosslyn Mountain Boys) run the musical and emotional gamut each night with tortured country ballads, authentic-sounding rockabilly and country rock. Lead singer Joe Triplett has the most captivating stage presence and style of any performer in the area.

On arrival in Washington, pick up a copy of *The Unicorn Times*, a free monthly. It's an impressive, highly readable and informative paper covering all the arts in the Washington area. There are gig listings and interesting articles on local musicians. When a big rock name comes to Washington they usually play the massive Capital Center on Harry S Truman Drive. In the summer many well known artists play the theater at Wolf Trap Farm Park. The Ontario Theater at 1700 Columbia Road NW brings in many of the new and up-and-coming national names.

CLUBS

Cellar Door, 1201 34th St. NW, 337-3389. Probably Washington's best-known club, consistently brings in top-notch acts, generally for two- or three- night stands. A wide variety of music.

Desperado's, 34th and M Sts. NW, 338-5220. Music nightly from 8:45. It's across the road from the Cellar Door and features the best of local talent.

HONKY TONKIN'

Blues Alley, rear of 1073 Wisconsin Ave. NW, 337-4141. One of the city's classiest night spots offers top-notch jazz ranging between traditional and mainstream. Sound is the clearest in town. Outstanding Creole cooking.

Mr. Henry's Tenley Circle, 4323 Wisconsin Ave. NW, 362-6079. You'll notice a string of clubs in the Washington area called Mr. Henry's. They have quite different musical policies. The Tenley Circle place is a showcase for up-and-coming rock bands.

Childe Harold, 1610 20th St. NW, 483-6702. Small club, holding little more than 100, that offers top-flight performers in all fields. New wave rock on Thursdays. Music from 9PM, cover varies and can be expensive.

Bayou, 3131 K St. NW, 333-2897. Big place that features local rock and occasional blues and jazz names.

Columbia Station, 1836 Columbia Rd. NW, 667-2900. Local rock. "Proper dress discouraged."

Pigfoot, 1812 Hamlin St. NE, 635-3888. Offers regular jazz bill in an intimate atmosphere.

One Step Down, 2517 Pennsylvania at 25th St., 331-8863. Across the street from where the White House staff celebrate happy hour is a small bar that features live jazz and has the only jazz jukebox in town.

Psychedelly, 4846 Cordell Ave., Bethesda, Maryland, 654-6611. Ordinary looking little club with a knack for booking the hottest local bands. Very popular at weekends.

Takoma Tap Room, 8210 Piney Branch Rd., Silver Spring, Maryland, 589-9764. Local talent.

Beacon's Backstage, Rt. 50 and Annandale Rd., Scenic Falls Church, Virginia, 533-9080. Live music every night except Mondays with local bands like Payday and talented blues aggregation, The Allstars.

Louie's Rock City, 3501 S. Jefferson St., Bailey's Crossroads,

Virginia, 379-6611. Local rock most nights and occasional national names. Club is across the road from a Korvettes store.

FESTIVALS

Festival of American Folklife held each summer on the National Mall, the 50-acre park between the Lincoln Memorial and the Washington Monument. Includes big name folk and blues artists.

National Folk Festival at Wolf Trap Farm Park, Vienna, Virginia. Ticket information: (703) 938-3800. A yearly tradition at Wolf Trap celebrated each July by scores of artists representing the lively and varied American music heritage. One of the finest festivals anywhere. Not only do the concerts present an astounding range of music of the Americas, the workshps provide a unique opportunity to get to know the musicians and craft folk intimately.

RECORD SHOPS

Road House Oldies, 958 Thayer Ave., Silver Spring, Maryland. Les Moskwitz runs this blues, R&B and rock 'n' roll store. He helps promote occasional concerts in town and is in touch with DC residents like Varetta Dillard and Bullmoose Jackson.

Hit and Run, 3808B Harvard Ave., Kensington, Maryland, 983-3500. Oldies from the sixties. This could be the place to pick up singles on local labels by bands like The Telstars, The Hangmen and Claude Jones. Some of the performers like Roy Buchanan later gained a national audience.

Sabin's Discount Records, 3212 Pennsylvania Ave. SE, 582-2000. Carries one of the largest jazz inventories in the country and has a knowledgeable staff who actually let you listen to records before you buy. This building also houses the *Radio Free Jazz* newspaper.

Bread and Roses Community Record Store, 1724 20th St. NW at Q St., 387-6264. Has a large selection of bluegrass and cut-out racks of jazz, rock, blues and the classics.

Soul Shack. Two stores situated near each other on G Street just west of 12th, and on F just east of 11th. Good for soul record deletions.

The Record and Tape Exchange, 3245 M St. NW, 337-7970 and at 8608 Baltimore Blvd., ¼ mile north of the University of Maryland on Rt. 1, 345-9338. Large number of second-hand records and deletions.

RECORD LABEL

Adelphi Records, P.O. Box 288, Silver Spring, Maryland 20907. Washington's biggest and best local label is Adelphi whose releases range from blues to jazz to folk/country. They've released several albums by the excellent Nighthawks, one by The Rosslyn Mountain Boys before they became Payday, and an album apiece from two bands from Charlottesville, Virginia, but now based in DC — The Allstars, a blues band, and Coup De Grass who describe their music as "rhythm and bluegrass."

(Special thanks to *Richard Harrington*)

BLUEGRASS CAPITAL

"Late-blooming fans of bluegrass, which is often referred to as Appalachian soul music, are amused to hear Washington, DC, described as the bluegrass capital of the country, mecca for slick pickers with an eye to tradition. Surely Nashville, or some other points south, but Washington? But if you go down to Nashville, you'll find some good pickers — Roland White of Country Gazette works out of that city — but for the most part, the musicians lean to contemporary country, but bluegrass only shows its face occasionally in Nashville. Other points south? How about Louisville, home of another bluegrass? How about the Midwest? How about the West Coast? No, the heart of the music, in terms of sheer musical activity, interest and diversity, is right here in the nation's capital.

"Why Washington one can rightly wonder? It may be a simple matter of geography according to some local bluegrass aficionados. This has always been a transitional city, halfway north if you're looking for somewhere better, halfway home if you've been disappointed. Going either way one has access to the mountains which are the natural breeding grounds of bluegrass musicians. If you stretch it, the further you go from this city the slicker things get. New York has its share of sophisticated pickers and everybody knows about those Nasvhille cats. But too much of the music is played by rote, and the mountains seem to be a source of rejuvenation, a point of rekindling, a return to the job of playing for the sake of making music not money.

"This does not mean that this city hasn't got its share of bluegrass slickers, but there seems a greater camaraderie among the players, and a subsequent amount of interchange, based on musical ideas. People jamming, people sitting in, that is what bluegrass is all about in Washington.

"In the early days people didn't differentiate much between bluegrass and country. A lot of people still don't, which is unfortunate. Bluegrass is to country, well, a bit like jazz is to pop. It's not that accurate an equation but then you should get the idea. The great folk boom of the early sixties brought forth seeds of pseudo bluegrass which wasn't a bad thing since a lot of people moved on to the real thing after realizing there must be more to the music than the Kingston Trio and The Tarriers . . . Bluegrass reached a much wider audience and a much younger audience. Perhaps more importantly, younger musicians were inspired to come up with innovative ideas, and the music became a challenge as well as a delight.

"Bluegrass fans are a breed apart. In terms of percentage, more of them actually play the music than support any other music style. This is the major appeal of the various festivals where some of the best picking goes on around dozens of trailers and tents, with musicians wandering in and out of various aggregations, sometimes playing just a few licks they've gotten down pat and moving on before someone comes up with a more challenging tune. The club scene is a microcosm of this larger scene with future musicians, congressional aides, PhDs, country people, soured rock 'n' rollers — all sitting side by side, tapping feet, and smiling an unnatural amount of the time.

"Other cities around the country are developing their own bluegrass scene, but many are just now where Washington was in the mid-sixties. Although there is still a great deal of traditional bluegrass here, new grass is also extremely popular. In the last few years a great many changes have occurred in the structure of the music, and the flow of enthusiasm may help it grow even more in the next few years. Even if there are modifications in the music, it's doubtful that bluegrass will give country or rock a run for its money. Its personalities are not that dominant and that seems to be important. Maybe it's one of the charms of the music. Clubs and small concerts will remain the best settings for bluegrass, which is ultimately an intimate music, shared among friends. It's nice that this city has become such a home for it."

Richard Harrington (reprinted with the permission of the author from an article in *Unicorn Times*)

CLUBS

Several clubs in the Washington area feature bluegrass on a regular basis. Check the monthly "Bluegrass and Old Timey" guide in *Unicorn Times*. The following is only a selection of the clubs.

Birchmere, 2723 Southwakefield St., Arlington, Virginia,

931-5058. The region's premier bluegrass nightspot. The Seldom Scene play here every Thursday night — get there early to be sure of a seat. The club has a good sound system and good sight lines.

DiGennaro's, corner of 197 and Contee Rd., Laurel, Maryland, (301) 953-3444. Regular bluegrass. On Thursdays Windfall; Fridays Foggy Bottom; Saturdays, different local bands.

Charlie's West Side, West Annapolis, Maryland, 263-8396. Popular place where The Grim Pickers, Coup de Grass and The Bluegrass Cardinals play regularly.

Partners Two, Centerville, Virginia. A country-rock spot that has frequent bluegrass gigs.

Shakey's Pizza Parlors. Several in this area feature bluegrass on a regular basis.

BLUEGRASS TALENT

The Seldom Scene could be world-famous and play to packed houses wherever they go — but they choose not to. They play the Birchmere once a week, do a few other gigs and the occasional festival. "It's still fun — it's not a job," explains Tommy Gray who still holds down a day job. The band members are Gray on bass, Mike Auldridge on dobro (the best known member of the band, he's played cameos on albums by Emmylou Harris and others), John Duffey on mandolin, Ben Eldridge on banjo and newest member Phil Rosenthal on guitar, banjo and mandolin. The Seldom Scene are an extremely talented and versatile bunch of quality musicians who can take much of the credit — or blame — for the increasing trend of changing bluegrass from a rural to a more urban music. Their repertoire includes songs by modern folk and country writers like Paul Craft and Herb Peterson. According to country music authority Douglas B. Green, "That's what bluegrass needed — an infusion of new songs. Basically a lot of musicians were hacks — are hacks. Bluegrass was in danger of becoming a stylized music which would grow stagnant like Dixieland jazz."

Coup de Grass come from Charlottesville, Virginia, but now call

Washington home. Their unusual bluegrass repertoire includes remarkable versions of forties swing classics and sixties R&B tunes.

The Bluegrass Cardinals are among America's most respected bluegrass outfits. Originally based in DC, they moved to California but have returned home and, though frequently on the road, they do make occasional appearances in the Washington area.

The Country Gentlemen are a bluegrass institution who've been performing for over 20 years. They're pioneers of the progressive bluegrass. **Dixie Grass** play traditional bluegrass, as do **Grass On The Rocks** while **Harlequin Mountain** are newcomers to the scene, playing "semi-progressive" and "easy listening" grass. **Foxfire** boasts two lady pickers and play mainly traditional music.

(Special thanks to *Richard Harrington* and *Robert Kyle*)

RADIO

Radio is in the hands of such a lot of fools
Trying to anaesthetize the way you feel
Elvis Costello, "Radio, Radio"
(Plangent Vision Music, Ltd., 1978)

There are over 50,000 FM and AM radio stations in America. A few are very good indeed but most suffer from remarkably unimaginative programming. The good-old days of loose-limbed, laid-back and unstructured FM radio have been replaced — rigid and homogenized playlists are the norm though many rock stations continue to call themselves "progressive." Singer Ry Cooder echoes the feelings of many when he commented on American radio in the *New Musical Express*: "The music I hear all sounds the same. When I was a kid in LA there was a hillbilly station, that was country and western period, it wasn't even Nashville music. Then there was a rhythm and blues station which was strictly R&B, none of this fancy hotshot stuff. Then there was a teenage station. Now you turn on a station and the whole damn radio sounds alike. I can't stand it!"

The program director of KSAN in San Francisco, one of the few big rock stations with a relatively unrestricted playlist, was quoted in *Rolling Stone* about the trend to safe radio: "Because of the competitive situation and because the stations must have a substantial piece of the audience in order to survive, they play those things they can be relatively sure will be hits, rather than take a chance and expose new product before it's tested." The major rock stations tend to play oldies and tracks from the best-selling albums of the day — a composite of sounds that writer Simon Frith has tagged "hip easy listening."

The following list of major rock stations does include some of the best, like KSAN in San Francisco, WNEW in New York (one of the first to play "new wave" records) and WBCN in Boston.

ALABAMA

Auburn	WFRI FM	97.7
Birmingham	WERC FM	106.9
Enterprise	WIRB FM	96.6
Huntsville	WAHR FM	99.1
Mobile	WABB FM	97.5
Montgomery	WKLH FM	92.3

ALASKA

Anchorage	KGOT FM	101.3

ARIZONA

Phoenix	KDKB FM	93.3
Tucson	KWFM FM	92.9

ARKANSAS

Fayetteville	KKEG FM	92.1
Ft. Smith	KISR FM	93.7
Little Rock	KLAZ FM	98.5

CALIFORNIA

Anaheim	KEZY FM	95.9
Bakersfield	KKXX FM	107.9
Carmel	KLRB FM	101.7
Escondido	Rock 92	
Eureka	KFMI FM	96.2
Fresno	Rock 96	
Indio	KRCQ FM	101.7
Los Angeles	KMET FM	94.7
Sacramento	KZAP FM	98.5
San Bernardino	KOLA FM	99.9
San Diego	KPRI FM	106.5
San Francisco	KSAN FM	94.9
San Jose	KOME FM	98.5
San Rafael	KTIM FM	100.9
Santa Barbara	KTYD FM	99.9
Santa Maria	KXFM FM	99

COLORADO

Breckinridge	KLGT FM	102.3
Denver	KAZY FM	106.7
Ft. Collins	KTCL FM	93.3
Glenwood Springs	KGLS FM	92.7

CONNECTICUT

Bridgeport	I 95 FM	
Hartford	WHCN FM	105.9

DELAWARE

Georgetown	WSEA FM	93.5

DISTRICT OF COLUMBIA

Washington	DC 101 FM	

FLORIDA

Ft. Lauderdale	WSHE FM	103.5
Gainesville	WGVL FM	105.5
Jacksonville	WAIV FM	96.9
Lehigh Acres	WSWF FM	107
Orlando	WDIZ FM	100.3
Panama City	WP FM	107.9
Sarosota/ St. Petersburg/ Tampa	WQSR FM	102.5
Tallahassee	WGLF FM	104

GEORGIA

Atlanta	WKLS FM	96
Augusta	WAUG FM	105.7
Columbus	WWRH FM	104.9
Gainesville	WFOX FM	97.1
Savannah	WZAT FM	102.1
Warner-Robins (Macon)	WRBN FM	101.7

HAWAII

Honolulu	KQMQ FM	93.1

IDAHO

Boise	KBBK FM	92.3
Pocatello	KSNN FM	96.1
Rexburg	KADQ FM	94.3

ILLINOIS

Carbondale	WIDB FM	104
Champaign	WPGU FM	107.1
Chicago	WXRT FM	93
Peoria	WWCT FM	105.7
Rockford	WYFE FM	95.3

INDIANA

Evansville	WKDQ FM	99.5
Ft. Wayne	WPTH FM	95.1
Indianapolis	WNAP FM	93.1
Lafayette	WAZY FM	96.7
South Bend	WRBR FM	103.9
Terre Haute	WVTS FM	100.7

IOWA

Des Moines/ Ames	KCCQ FM	107.1
Iowa City	KICG FM	100.7

Mason City	KLSS FM	106
Sioux City	KSEZ FM	97.9

KANSAS

Hays	KJLS FM	103.3
Salina	KSKG FM	93.7
Wichita	KEYN FM	103.7

KENTUCKY

Ashland	WAMX FM	94
Henderson	WKDQ FM	99.5
Lexington	WKQQ FM	98.1
Louisville	WLRS FM	102.3
Paducah	WPAD FM	96.9

LOUISIANA

Baton Rouge	WFMF FM	102.5
Lafayette	KPEL FM	99.9
Lake Charles	KGRA FM	104
Monroe	KNOE FM	101.9
New Orleans	WRNO FM	99.5
Shreveport	KROK FM	94.5
Thibodaux	KXOR FM	106.3

MAINE

Lewiston	WBLM FM	107.5
Orono	WMEB FM	91.9
Presque Island	WDHP FM	96.9

MARYLAND

Baltimore	WIYY FM	97.9
Frederick	WZYQ FM	104

MASSACHUSETTS

Boston	WBCN FM	104.1
Springfield	WAQY FM	102.1
Worcester	WAAF FM	107.3

MICHIGAN

Big Rapids	WBRN FM	100.9
Detroit	WABX FM	99.5
Flint	WWCK FM	105.5
Grand Rapids	WLAV FM	97
Ishpeming	WJPD FM	92.3
Lansing	WVIC FM	94.9
Marquette	WBKX FM	105

MINNESOTA

Duluph	WAKX FM	98.9
Minn./St. Paul	KQRS FM	92.5
Pipestone	KLOH FM	98.7

MISSISSIPPI

Jackson	WZZQ FM	102.9
Laurel	WNSL FM	100.3
Meridian	WALT FM	97
Natchez	WQNZ FM	94.1

MISSOURI

Branson	KIRK FM	106.3
Columbia	KFMZ FM	98.3
Greenfield/ Springfield	KRFG FM	93.5
Kansas City	KY	102
St. Louis	KSHE FM	94.7
Sedalla	KCBW FM	92.1

MONTANA

Anaconda	KGLM FM	97.7
Billings	Y 9 3	
Great Falls	KNUW FM	95
Missoula	KYLT FM	100.1

NEBRASKA

Columbus	KTTT FM	93.5
Omaha	KQKQ FM	98.5

NEVADA

Reno	KGLR FM	105.7

NEW HAMPSHIRE

Conway	WBNC FM	93.5

NEW JERSEY

Princeton	WPRB FM	103.3

NEW MEXICO

Alamagordo	KYLO FM	90
Albuquerque	KMYR FM	99.5
Las Cruces	KASK FM	103.1

NEW YORK

Albany	WQBK FM	104
Buffalo	WGRQ FM	96.9
Elmira	WXXY FM	104.9
Ithaca	WVBR FM	93.5
New York	WNEW FM	102.7
Poughkeepsie	WPDH FM	101.5
Rochester	WCMF FM	96.5
Utica/Syracuse	WOUR FM	96.9

NORTH CAROLINA

Charlotte	WROQ FM	95
Durham	WDBS FM	107.1
Farmville	WRQR FM	94.3
Greensboro	WRQK FM	98.7

NORTH DAKOTA

Fargo	KQWB FM	98.7
Grand Forks	KKXL FM	92.9
Minot	KCJB FM	97.1

OHIO

Athens	ACRN FM	99.3
Bellaire (Wheeling)	WOMP FM	100.5
Bellevue	WNNR FM	92.1
Cincinnati	WEBN FM	102.7
Cleveland	WMMS FM	100.7
Columbus	WCOL FM	92.3
Dayton	WVUD FM	99.9
Jackson	WCJO FM	97.7
Toledo	WMHE FM	92.5
Youngstown	WSRD FM	101

OKLAHOMA

Lawton	KRLG	98FM
Oklahoma City	KATT FM	100
Ponca City	KLOR FM	99.3
Tulsa	KMOD FM	97.5

OREGON

Bend	KXIQ FM	94.1
Eugene	KZEL FM	96.9
Portland	KGON FM	92.3

PENNSYLVANIA

Erie	WMDI FM	102.3
Linesville	WVCC FM	101.7
Philadelphia	WMMR	FM
93.3		
Pittsburgh	WYDD FM	104.7
Lancaster/ Starview/ York	WRHY FM	92.7
Scranton/ Wilkes-Barre	WEZX FM	107

SOUTH CAROLINA

Charleston	WWWZ FM	93.5
Myrtle Beach	WKZQ FM	101.7

SOUTH DAKOTA

Vermillion	KVRF FM	102.3
Watertown	KIXX FM	96.1

TENNESSEE

Chattanooga	KWXW FM	106.9
Jackson	WKIR FM	104
Johnson City	WQUT FM	101.5
Memphis	WMC FM	100
Nashville	WKDF FM	103.3
Oak Ridge/ Knoxville	WOKI FM	103.3

TEXAS

Austin	KLBJ FM	93.7
Corpus Christi	KNCN FM	101.3
Dallas	KZEW FM	98
El Paso	KPAS FM	93.7
Houston	KLOL FM	101.1
Lubbock	LKBK FM	94.5
McAllen/ Brownsville	KB FM	104.1
San Angelo	KIXY FM	93.1
Tyler	KTYL FM	93.1

UTAH

Logan	KVWJ FM	94

VERMONT

Stowe	WRFB FM	101.7

VIRGINIA

Blacksburg	WVVV FM	105
Norfolk/ Virginia Beach	WMYK FM	94
Richmond	WRXL FM	102.1

WASHINGTON

Bellingham	KISM FM	93
Longview	KLYK FM	105.5
Seattle	KISW FM	99.9
Spokane	KHQ FM	98.1
Yakima	KIT FM	94.5

WEST VIRGINIA

Charleston	WVAF FM	100
Morgantown	WCLG FM	100
Parkersburg	WIBZ FM	99.3

WISCONSIN

Eau Claire	WBIZ FM	100.7
Green Bay	WIXX FM	101.1
La Crosse	WSPL FM	95.9
Madison	WIBA FM	101.5
Milwaukee	93-QFM	
Wausau	WIFC FM	95.5

WYOMING

Casper	KAWY FM	94.5
Gillette	KOLL FM	93.5
Laramie	KIOZ FM	102.9

While you'll find the big rock stations in the middle of your radio's FM band — usually between 92 and 104 — more interesting and unusual sounds can often be tracked down at either end. Most big towns have college stations where the music varies dramatically according to the DJ's who can be very good but often unbelievably self-indulgent, laid back and into avant-garde jazz. The programming on the National Public Radio affiliates is much more consistent. Member stations of National Public Radio are noncommercial and the nearest equivalent to Britain's excellent BBC Radio Four. There are some good music programs, notably "Folk Festival USA" every Saturday afternoon which consists of taped highlights of blues, folk, bluegrass and country festivals across the country. A list of National Public Radio stations follows.

ALABAMA

Birmingham	WBHM FM	90.3
Gadsden	WEXP FM	88.9
Huntsville	WLRH FM	89.3

ALASKA

Bethel	KYUK AM	580
Fairbanks	KUAC FM	104.,
Kotzebue	KOTZ AM	720

ARIZONA

Phoenix	KMCR FM	91.5
Tucson	KUAT AM	1550
	KUAT FM	90.5
Yuma	KAWC AM	1320

ARKANSAS

Jonesboro	KASU FM	91.9

CALIFORNIA

Long Beach	KLON FM	88.1
Los Angeles	KUSC FM	91.5
Northridge	KCSN FM	88.5
Pasadena	KPCS FM	89.3
San Bernardino	KVCR FM	91.9
San Diego	KPBS FM	89.5
San Francisco	KALW FM	91.7
	KQED FM	88.5
San Mateo	KCSM FM	91.1
Santa Monica	KCRW FM	89.9
Santa Rosa	KBBF FM	89.1
Santa Rosa	KBBF FM	89.1
Stockton	KUOP FM	91.3

COLORADO

Denver	KCFR FM	90.1
Greeley	KUNC FM	91.5

DISTRICT OF COLUMBIA

	WAMU FM	88.5
	WETA FM	90.9

FLORIDA

Boynton Beach	WHRS FM	91.7
Jacksonville	WJCT FM	89.9
Miami	WLRN FM	91.3
Panama City	WKGC FM	90.7
Tallahassee	WFSU FM	91.5
Tampa	WUSF FM	89.7

GEORGIA		
Atlanta	WABE FM	91.9
ILLINOIS		
Carbondale	WSIU FM	91.9
Chicago	WBEZ FM	91.5
De Kalb	WNIU FM	89.5
Edwardsville	WSIE FM	88.7
Peoria	WCBU FM	89.9
Springfield	WSSR FM	91.9
Urbana	WILL AM	580
INDIANA		
Bloomington	WFIU FM	103.7
Indianapolis	WIAN FM	90.1
Vincennes	WVUB FM	91.1
West Lafayette	WBAA AM	920
IOWA		
Ames	WOI AM	640
	WOI FM	90.1
Cedar Falls	KHKE FM	89.5
	KUNI	90.9
Cedar Rapids	KCCK FM	88.3
Iowa City	WSUI AM	910
	KSUI FM	91.7
KANSAS		
Lawrence	KANU FM	91.5
Manhattan	KSAC AM	580
Wichita	WMUW FM	89.1
KENTUCKY		
Lexington	WBKY FM	91.3
Louisville	WFPL FM	89.3
	WFPK FM	91.9
	WUOL FM	90.5
Morehead	WMKY FM	90.3
Murray	WKMS FM	91.3
Richmond	WEKU FM	88.9
LOUISIANA		
New Orleans	WWNO FM	89.9
MAINE		
Bangor	WMEH FM	90.9
Portland	WMEA FM	90.1
MARYLAND		
Baltimore	**WBJC FM**	**91.5**
	WEAA FM	**88.9**
Takoma Park	**WGTS FM**	**91.9**
MASSACHUSETTS		
Amherst	WFCR FM	88.5
Boston	WBUR FM	90.9
	WGBH FM	89.7
MICHIGAN		
Ann Arbor	WFCR FM	88.5
Berrien Springs	WAUS FM	90.9
Detroit	WDET FM	101.9
East Lansing	WKAR AM	870
Flint	WFBE FM	95.1
Grand Rapids	WVGR FM	104.1
Houghton	WGGL FM	91.1
Interlochen	WIAA FM	88.3
Kalamazoo	WMUK FM	102.1
Marquette	WNMU FM	90.1
Mt. Pleasant	WCMU FM	89.5
MINNESOTA		
Collegeville	KSJR FM	90.1
Duluth	WSCD FM	92.9
Grand Rapids	KAXE FM	91.9
Minneapolis/ St. Paul	KSJN FM	91.1
Minneapolis	KUAM AM	770
Moorhead	KCCM FM	91.1
Northfield	WCAL AM	770
	WCAL FM	89.3
Pipestone	KRSW FM	91.7
Rushford	KLSE FM	91.7
MISSISSIPPI		
Senatobia	WNJC FM	90.1
MISSOURI		
Buffalo	KBFL FM	90.3
Columbia	KBIA FM	91.3
Jefferson City	KLUM FM	88.9
Kansas City	KCUR FM	89.3
Maryville	KXCV FM	90.5
Point Lookout	KSOZ FM	91.7
Rolla	KUMR FM	88.5
Springfield	KSMU FM	91.1
St. Louis	KWMU FM	90.7
Warrensburg	KCMW FM	90.9
MONTANA		
Missoula	KUFM FM	89.1

NEBRASKA

Omaha	KIOS FM	91.5

NEW JERSEY

Newark	WBGO FM	88.3

NEW MEXICO

Albuquerque	KIPC FM	91.5
Las Cruces	KRWG FM	90.7
Ramah	KTDB FM	89.7

NEW YORK

Albany	WAMC FM	90.3
Binghamton	WSKG FM	89.3
Buffalo	WBFO FM	88.7
	WEBR AM	970
	WNED FM	94.5
Canton	WSLU FM	96.7
New York City	WNYC AM	830
	WNYC FM	93.9
Oswego	WRVO FM	89.9
Rocchester	WXXI FM	91.5
Schenectady	WMHT FM	89.1
Syracuse	WCNY FM	91.3

NORTH CAROLINA

Chapel Hill	WUNC FM	91.5
Warrenton	WVSP FM	90.9
Winston-Salem	WFDD FM	88.5

NORTH DAKOTA

Belcourt	KEYA FM	88.5
Fargo	KDSU FM	91.9
Grand Forks	KFJM AM	1370
	KFJM FM	89.3

OHIO

Athens	WOUB AM	1340
	WOUB FM	91.3
Cincinnati	WGUC FM	90.9
Cleveland	WBOE FM	90.3
Columbus	WCBE FM	90.5
	WOSU AM	820
	WOSU FM	89.7
Kent	WKSU FM	89.7
Oxford	WMUB FM	88.5
Toledo	WGTE FM	91.3
Wilberforce	WCSU FM	88.9
Yellow Springs	WYSO FM	91.5
Youngstown	WYSU FM	88.5

OKLAHOMA

Stillwater	KOSU FM	91.7

OREGON

Corvallis	KOAC AM	550
Eugene	KLCC FM	90.3
	KWAX FM	91.1
Portland	KBOO FM	90.7
	KBPS AM	1450
	KOAP FM	91.5

PENNSYLVANIA

Erie	WQLN FM	91.3
Hershey	WITF FM	89.5
Philadelphia	WUHY FM	90.9
Pittsburgh	WDUQ FM	90.5
	WQED FM	89.3
Scranton	WVIA FM	89.9

PUERTO RICO

Hato Rey	WIPR AM	940
	WIPR FM	91.3

SOUTH CAROLINA

Charleston	WSCI FM	89.3
Columbia	WLTR FM	91.3
Greenville	WEPR FM	90.1
Sumter	WMPR FM	88.1

SOUTH DAKOTA

Brookings	KSED FM	88.3
Vermillion	KUSD FM	690
	KUSD FM	89.9

TENNESSEE

Collegedale	WSMC FM	90.7
Johnson City	WETS FM	89.5
Knoxville	WUOT FM	91.9
Memphis	WKNO FM	91.1
Murfreesboro	WMOT FM	89.5
Nashville	WPLN FM	90.3

TEXAS

Austin	KUT FM	90.7
Beaumont	KVLU FM	91.3
College Station	KAMU FM	90.3
Commerce	KETR FM	88.9
Dallas	KERA FM	90.1
El Paso	KTEP FM	88.5
Houston	KPFT FM	90.1
Killeen	KNCT FM	91.3

HONKY TONKIN'

UTAH

Logan	KUSU FM	91.5
Provo	WBYU FM	88.9
Salt Lake City	KUER FM	90.1

VIRGINIA

Harrisonburg	WMRA FM	90.7
Norfolk	WTGM FM	89.5
Richmond	WRFK FM	106.5
Roanoke	WVWR FM	89.1

WASHINGTON

Pullman	KWSU AM	1250
Seattle	KRAB FM	107.7
	KUOW FM	94.9
Tacoma	KTOY FM	91.7

WEST VIRGINIA

Beckley	WVPB FM	91.7
Buckhannon	WVPW FM	91.7

WISCONSIN

Auburndale	WLBL AM	930
Brule	WHSA FM	89.9
Colfax	WHWC FM	88.3
Delafield	WHAD FM	90.7
Green Bay	WPNE FM	89.3
Highland	WHHI FM	91.3
Kenosha	WGTD FM	91.1
La Crescent	WHLA FM	90.3
La Crosse	WLSU FM	88.9
Madison	WERN FM	88.7
	WHA AM	970
Milwaukee	WUWM FM	89.7
Wausau	WHRM FM	91.9

WDBS fm107

WIOQ 102 FM

WNYC TV31 FM94 AM830

RECORDS AND RECORD BUYING

SMALL RECORD LABELS

In this section I'll be listing some of the small and specialist record labels that I haven't managed to fit into the area-by-area listings. A detailed and comprehensive guide to small American record labels would run for many pages and probably make a book. What follows is only a selection.

Some of the small labels have been established for years and have large catalogues while others are very new and small, sometimes started by a single musician as an outlet for his work. The labels tend to have one thing in common — poor distribution and therefore low sales. The record industry works for the benefit of the huge corporate conglomerates for whom making money is more important than making music — for the small labels the reverse is usually true. They need and deserve your support.

Flying Fish, 1304 W. Shubert, Chicago, Illinois 60614. One of the very best small labels with great artists like Mike Auldridge (see Washington Bluegrass chapter), John Hartford, The Red Clay Ramblers, Tracy Nelson, Norman Blake, New Grass Revival and Buddy Emmons. Flying Fish distributes Mountain Railroad Records (who release Chicago folk albums), Nessa and Kaleidoscope Records.

Delmark Records, 4243 N. Lincoln, Chicago, Illinois 60618. Another Chicago-based record label with a long established reputation for issuing fine albums. They specialize in blues and jazz and Delmark artists include Junior Wells, Jimmy Dawkins, Otis Rush, Sun Ra, Sonny Stitt and George Lewis.

Red Lightnin', 517 Eastern Avenue, Ilford, Essex 1G2 6LT, England. Peter Shertser's little post-war blues label now has over 15 titles on catalogue. Clarence "Gatemouth" Brown's "San Antonio Ballbuster" and Ike Turner's "Kings of Rhythm" are particularly recommended.

Charly Records, 9 Beadon Rd., London W6 OEA, England. Charly issues wonderful rock 'n' roll and blues albums. They have the rights to the legendary Sun catalogue and have reissued most of the recordings made in Memphis by artists like Jerry Lee Lewis, Carl Perkins and others. Send stamps or International Reply Coupons to Charly for a copy of their catalogue.

Arhoolie Records, 10341 San Pablo Ave., El Cerrito, California. Wonderful label that covers country blues, piano blues, Louisiana Zydeco, traditional and modern jazz, religious and gospel, folk, Tex-Mex, country, old-timey and Western swing.

Folkways Records, 43 W. 63rd St., New York City, NY 10023. Folkways has the most extensive selection of folk music in the world. They have been going since around 1950 and have never deleted any of their albums. They cover just about every aspect of folk music — traditional, contemporary, blues, jazz, bluegrass, old-timey, ethnic.

County Records. County issues beautifully packaged albums of classic country music and contemporary recordings of old-time and bluegrass.

Rounder Records, 186 Willow Ave., Somerville, Massachusetts 02144. Rounder has an outstanding catalogue of bluegrass recordings; historical re-issues from the thirties through to modern albums by the likes of Norman Blake, Don Stover and the popular New England outfit Joe Val and the New England Bluegrass Boys; country blues and ethnic recordings from the US and England. Rounder's biggest sellers are the records of George Thorogood and the Destroyers, a white blues band.

Philo Records, The Barn, North Ferrisburg, Vermont 05473. Each Philo record cover bears the legend "Philo Records encourages the artists to assume full creative control of his or her album. This album is conceived by the artist." Philo Records and its recording studio Earth Audio Techniques are located in an old weathered barn on the southern slopes of Mount Philo, just north of Burlington, Vermont. They record a variety of artists in the folk idiom, including Mary McCaslin and Jim Ringer, David Van Ronk and The Boys of the Lough. Although the resident staff contribute ideas and technical knowledge, the artists always have the last word. Fretless Records is a sister label to Philo that functions as a co-operative venture for lesser known performers which enables them to "have product."

Sierra-Briar, PO Box 5853, Pasadena, California 91107. West Coast bluegrass and country rock.

GNP Crescendo Records, 8560 Sunset Boulevard, Suite 603, Los Angeles, California 90069. Diverse catalog includes two albums by the excellent zydeco group Queen Ida and her Bon Temps Band.

Yazoo. Excellent blues label with albums by Tampa Red, Blind Willie McTell, Charlie Patton and the Reverend Gary Davis.

Stash Records, PO Box 390, Brooklyn, New York 11215. Stash Records were founded in 1975 by Bernard Brightman who explains: "The label is motivated by an appreciation of Afro-American music and its contribution to American life. Most of the releases have been based upon contemporary concepts translated into the jazz idiom. The area of drugs, homosexuality, women in jazz, and humor form the major part of the catalogue. The label is willing to accept challenges which do not necessarily have commercial appeal and failures are not measured in dollars." Two Stash albums, "Reefer Songs" and "Copulating Blues," are particularly recommended.

If you're involved with a small record label that isn't listed here, please write with details to the editorial address.

WHERE TO FIND RECORDS ON SMALL LABELS

Many releases on the more established small labels — like Rounder, Arhoolie and Folkways — are listed in the *Schwann Record and Tape Guide* (the home reference guide to recorded music(and can be ordered from most record retailers, but many people prefer to buy from mail order dealers who specialize in small labels. Four American dealers who've proved reliable in the past are listed below.

Down Home Music, Inc., 10341 San Pablo Ave., El Cerrito, California 94350, Tel: (415) 525-1494. They stock just about every worthwhile blues, bluegrass, old-timey, folk, traditional jazz and ethnic record release still on catalogue from small companies all over the world. They also have one of the best record shops in the US — see San Francisco chapter.

Brother Slim's Record Revival, 7121 W. Vickery, No. 118, Fort Worth, Texas 76126. They specialize in off-the-wall and hard-to-find albums and books. They are particularly good for blues, jazz, Cajun, Western swing, old-timey, Tex-Mex and bluegrass.

Roundup Records, PO Box 474, Somerville, Massachusetts 02144. The mail order arm of Rounder Records stocks a wide range of blues, bluegrass, old-timey and Cajun. Send at least $1 for their latest catalogue.

Cross Country, PO Box 3584, Washington, DC 20007. Run by Bruce Rosenstein who writes the best "import records" column in any American paper (for the Washington monthly *Unicorn Times*). Cross Country specializes in hard-to-find records and publications. They have import albums, singles, EPs and local records and publications. They also have a good selection of cut-out and over-stock albums, and domestic and imported fan magazines and rock publications.

In Britain there's **Mike's Country Music Room**, 18 Hilton Avenue, Aberdeen, Scotland, Tel: (0224) 44776. Mike is the leading European mail order dealer and distributor specializing in old-time country music, bluegrass and steel guitar albums from the US. Send for a free list of over 1000 choice albums. **G.I. Records**, 30B Raeburn Place, Edinburgh, E14 1HN, Scotland, are very good for progressive country music and stock several albums on small American labels. **Richard Wootton**, the editor of this book, runs a mail order service for British and European customers, from 21 Melbourne Court, Anerley Road, Penge, London SE 20, England. The catalogue is selective and aimed not so much at collectors as record buyers wishing to sample different American music forms — the best of blues, Cajun, zydeco, bluegrass, rock 'n' roll and country music. Send stamps or International Reply Coupons for free lists.

RECORD COLLECTING

Finding details of the best stores and warehouses for rare records has not been easy. Record collectors are understandably secretive about good places because they fear that publicity will dry up their sources. A fair bit of detective work is therefore necessary. On arrival in a new town, I'd always recommend checking the yellow pages first and visiting the stores that claim to specialize in rare records. Talk to the people in the store — on both sides of the counter — and follow their leads and advice.

Cities like New York and Los Angeles have dozens of oldies stores where it's probably possible to find almost any record you've ever wanted. However, the price you'll have to pay will probably be high and beyond your means. It's best to visit other cities where people are less knowledgeable about records and their value and have lower overheads. I've found Philadelphia, Washington, Chicago, Detroit and Dallas/Fort Worth among the best cities for record buying.

ARHOOLIE RECORDS
ARHOOLIE FOLKLYRIC BLUES CLASSICS OLD TIMEY
DOWN HOME MUSIC SINCE 1960

the Record Hunter
EST. 1945

KING KAROL

SAM GOODY, INC.

FESTIVALS

Festivals are highly recommended as a source of good music in pleasant surroundings and also as an important alternative to the bland homogeneity of mass entertainment. There are hundreds of festivals throughout the United States with most taking place in the summer months. Some are specifically musical, others use music as a supplement to the main attraction.

Bluegrass fans should check the April issue of the monthly magazine *Bluegrass Unlimited* which lists the main festivals each year. *Living Blues* magazine does its best to list the forthcoming blues festivals. Cancellations and delays are uncommon, especially with the long established events, but they do sometimes occur and you're strongly advised to write or call festival directors or local authorities before setting out on long journeys.

What follows is a list of some of the bigger and best known American festivals. Specific dates can be obtained by writing to the contact indicated after each individual listing.

January

National Western Stock Show, Denver, Colorado. One of the nation's biggest rodeos and livestock shows. The nine-day show held in mid-January includes musical entertainment. National Western Stock Show, 1325 E. 46th Ave., Denver, Colorado.

February

Washington Birthday Celebration, Laredo, Texas. The oldest and largest fiesta on the entire Mexican border. Four days of revelry in the middle of the month. Mrs. Mary Lou Berrera, Washington Birthday Association, Sames-Moore Bldg., Laredo, TX 78040.

Houston Livestock Show and Rodeo, Houston, Texas. The biggest names in country music are featured at one of the nation's outstanding rodeos. Dick Weekley, Houston Livestock Show and Rodeo,

PO Box 20070, Houston, TX 77025.

Mardi Gras, New Orleans. There are parades and parties for the 10 days prior to Mardi Gras — traditionally the last day of wining and dining before the fasting for Lent. New Orleans Tourist Information Center, 334 Royal St., New Orleans, LA 70130.

Mardi Gras Day, Mobile, Alabama. This is the city that originated Mardi Gras over 200 years ago. In the weeks before, there are several parades and parties. Bill Damouy, PO Box 2407, Mobile, AL 36601.

March

Country-Western Jamboree, Dickinson, North Dakota. Annual battle of the bands in late March where state and regional country bands compete for prizes. O.T. Belsheim, Dickinson State College, Dickinson, ND 58601.

April

Strawberry Festival, Ponchatoula, Louisiana. Annual festival that salutes spring. A weekend of strawberry eating, frog jumping, square dancing and more. Strawberry Festival, PO Box 446, Ponchatoula, LA 70454.

World Champion Old-Time Fiddler's Convention, Union Grove, North Carolina. Three days in mid-April. Attracts musicians and stompers from all over the US. Here you can watch and participate in the unique Appalachian folk dance called clogging, in addition to hearing some great country music. J. Pierce Van Hoy, P.O. Box 38, Union Grove, NC 28689.

San Diego Folk Festival, SDSU Campus, San Diego, California. Recommended for its wide range of music from folk, country, Western swing to raw rockabilly. A real bargain. Lou Curtiss, Folk Arts Rare Records, 3611 Adams Ave., San Diego, CA 92112.

Arkansas Folk Festival and Crafts Show, Mountain View, Arkansas. The old-time music of the hills, handed down from one generation to the next, is played and sung at the Folk Center and at Courthouse Square. Two weekends in the latter half of the month. Jack Quaill, General Manager, Ozark Folk Center, Mountain View, AR, 72560.

Fiesta San Antonio, San Antonio, Texas. Gigantic fiesta in late April. Davis Burnett, Fiesta, San Antonio Commission, 316 N. Presa, San Antonio, TX 78205.

New Orleans Jazz and Heritage Festival, New Orleans. Wonderful — see New Orleans chapter for full details. Festival, PO Box 2530, New Orleans, LA 70130.

Oklahoma City Festival of the Arts, Oklahoma City, Oklahoma. Six days of fun and festivities in late April. Plenty of music and dancing. Arts Council, 3014 Paseo, Oklahoma City, OK 73106.

World's Largest Fish Fry, Paris, Tennessee. Tons of fresh catfish are cooked continuously for this annual event in the last week of the month. There's a rodeo, parade, carnival and square dancing. Paris-Henry County Chamber of Commerce, Paris, TN 38242.

KERRVILLE
FOLK
FESTIVAL

AZZ
FESTIVAL

May

Contraband Days, Lake Charles, Louisiana. Four days of dancing, parades, sail boat racing, Cajun music and food celebrating the era of pirates and buried treasure. Lake Charles/Calcasieu Tourist and Convention Committee, PO Box 1912 Lake Charles, LA 70601.

Mai Fest, Leavenworth, Washington. German music festival with dancing, an Ooompah band and food. Leavenworth Chamber of Commerce, PO Box 281, Leavenworth, WA 98826.

Pittsburgh Folk Festival, Pittsburgh, Pennsylvania. Three-day event with over 20 different ethnic groups performing in folk song and dance. Pittsburgh Folk Festival, 610 Fifth Ave., Pittsburgh, PA 15219.

Florida Folk Festival, White Springs, Florida. Festival in late May that helps keep alive age-old folk arts. Thelma Boltin, Stephen Foster Center, White Springs, FL 32096.

Kerrville Folk Festival, Kerrville, Texas. A long weekend in late May, featuring some of the finest folk and new country singers in Texas. Rod Kennedy, PO Box 1466, Kerrville, TX 78028.

June

West Virginia State Folk Festival, Glenville, West Virginia. The area's strong mountain heritage is expressed in hill music, bluegrass and the playing of the dulcimer. Fern Rollyson, Box 127, Glenville, WV 26351.

The Bluegrass Music Festival of the United States, Louisville, Kentucky. This is one of the largest outdoor, free music festivals. Three days in early June. Louisville Central Area Inc., 2125 Citizens Plaza, Louisville, KY 40202.

Annual Inter-Tribal Powwow, Albuquerque, New Mexico. One of the largest gatherings of tribes in the Southwest. Albuquerque Chamber of Commerce, 401 Second NW, Albuquerque, NM 87102.

Alaska Festival of Music, Anchorage, Alaska. Music in America's largest state tends to be a bit thin on the ground with the exception of this 15-day event in the first half of June each year. All kinds of good music. Betsy Raleigh, PO Box 325, Anchorage 99510.

Music City Fan Fare, Nashville, Tennessee. Special week for the country fans in early June. See the Music City chapter for full details.

Juneteenth Blues Festival, Houston, Texas. One of the best annual blues festivals in the US. See Houston chapter for details.

Beanblossom Bluegrass Festival, Beanblossom, Indiana. Weeklong fest held at the Brown County Jamboree Barn and Park. Bill Monroe, 3819 Dickerson Pike, Nashville, TN 37207.

June Festival of Mountain Folks' Music, Silver Dollar City, Missouri. Annual fest in early June that features 100 non-professional Ozark music-makers performing traditional mountain music. Chamber of Commerce, Silver Dollar City, MO 65616.

Ragtime Festival, St. Louis, Missouri. Prominent Dixieland musicians and ragtime bands perform aboard the Goldenrod Showboat on the Mississippi River and around the city. Convention and Visitors Bureau of Greater St. Louis, 500 Broadway Bldg., St. Louis, MO 63102.

National Hollerin' Contest, Spivey's Corner, North Carolina. Revives the art of hollerin', a traditional custom in rural areas where farmers would holler to their neighbors two miles away. Also chicken dinners, competitions, a hoe-down and a talent show. Mid-June. Ermon Godwin, Box 332, Dunn, NC 28334.

St. Louis Stassenfest, St. Louis, Missouri. Authentic oom-pa-pa bands, bratwurst, pretzels and other German food and entertainment, plus dancing and cultural events. Held in the area bounded by 15th, Market and Olive Streets. Convention and Visitors Bureau, 500 N. Broadway, St. Louis, MO 63102.

Newport Jazz Festival. America's best-known jazz festival is held at several locations in New York City and at Saratoga Springs, New York, and Stanhope Village, New Jersey. Late June. Charles

Bourgeoris, Newport Jazz Festival, 311 W. 74th, New York, NY 10023.

Singing on the Mountain, Grandfather Mountain, North Carolina. Long established all-day gospel singing and preaching fair. Lots of mountain music. Sunday in late June. Dick Barkley, Box 395, Linville, NC 28646.

Bavarian Summer Festival, Barnesville, Pennsylvania. Large scale festival features German food, beer and music in huge quantities. Held over a fortnight at the end of June and beginning of July at Lakewood Park in the Pennsylvania Highlands. There's all-day, non-stop music and dancing to German-American and Bavarian bands in the German Beer Hall. Kermit Dietrich, RD 2, Kempton, PA 19529.

Summerfest, Milwaukee, Wisconsin. A 10-day festival in late June with nationally known groups performing folk, rock, country and jazz. Wisconsin Division of Tourism, 123 W. Washington, Madison, WI 53702.

July

Old Time Fiddler's Jamboree, Smithville, Tennessee. Large scale festival with gospel, folk and country music plus harmonica and fiddling contests. Smithville Chamber of Commerce, Smithville, TN 37166.

Old Time Fiddler's Contest, Craftsbury Common, Vermont. Top fiddlers compete in a popular festival at this tiny village. Vermont Development Agency, 61 Elm Street, Montpelier, VT 05602.

August

Mountain Dance and Folk Festival, Asheville, North Carolina. One of the oldest and most colorful American festivals. Fiddlers, mountain pickers, ballad singers, dulcimer players, clog and square dancing. Asheville Chamber of Commerce, PO Box 1011, Asheville, NC 28802.

RCA Rodeo, Sidney, Iowa. The largest outdoor rodeo in the US. Top name cowboy performers and country stars. Sidney Rodeo, Sidney, IA 15652.

Texas Folklife Festival, San Antonio, Texas. Highly recommended event in early August. A composite of traditional folk performances, costumes, games, contests, demonstrations, crafts, art, food and music of the many ethnic groups contributing to Texas culture. Sandra Mintz, Texas Folklife Festival, Institute of Texas Cultures, PO Box 1226, San Antonio, TX 78294.

Old Fiddlers Convention, Galax, Virginia. Long established festival held in Felts Park near the scenic Blue Ridge Parkway. Galax Chamber of Commerce, PO Box 1006, Galax, VA 24333.

Philadelphia Folk Festival. Held in Pool's Farm, Upper Salford Township, near Schwenksville. A three-day event in the third week of August. Concerts with big name folk singers and workshops, dance sessions and campfire singing. Philadelphia Folksong Society, 7113 Emlen St., Philadelphia, PA 19119.

Minnesota State Fair, St. Paul, Minnesota. One of the nation's largest state fairs. The usual agricultural machinery displays, demolition derbies and a rodeo, plus concerts from nationally known acts. Minnesota State Fair, c/o State Capitol, St. Paul, MN 55013.

Michigan State Fair, Detroit, Michigan. Another very big state fair. Ten days at the end of August. Michigan State Fair Grounds, Detroit, MI 48232.

Annual International Folk Festival, Vernon Valley, New Jersey. Food, music, dancing and crafts of several countries. Barbara Harrison, Public Relations Director, Vernon Valley, NY 07462.

September

National Flatpicking Championship, Winfield, Kansas. Bluegrass event in mid-September. Walnut Valley Association, Inc., PO Box 245, Winfield, KS 67156.

October

State Fair of Texas, Dallas, Texas. America's largest state fair lasts for three weeks with top notch entertainment every night. Wayne Gallagher, PO Box 26010, Dallas, TX 75226.

Texas Prison Rodeo, Huntsville Prison, Texas. This rodeo originally started as a recreational program for the prisoners in 1932. Since then it has become a nationally-known event that draws 90,000 people for the four Sundays of October. Inmate contestants provide constant rodeo thrills, and top flight entertainers perform. Public Affairs Office, Texas Department of Corrections, PO Box 99, Huntsville, TX 77340.

BACKGROUND READING

Many of the best magazines and newspapers that will guide you to good music are regional and listed in relevant chapters. A number of national and specialist magazines can't be pinned down to a specific area and are listed here. A few are easy to find on almost any big city newsstand, others are much harder to track down.

There are hundreds of small magazines, usually available only by mail order, that turn up, usually at erratic intervals, in all parts of the US. Some of these are "fanzines" and usually make for very entertaining reading. A fanzine is usually written by an enthusiastic amateur and his/her friends and consists of a storehouse of trivial though sometimes fascinating information on a variety of cult heroes or specialist music forms. There are too many to list here and a lot would be gone by the time you read this, but both *Bomp* and *Goldmine* (see below) do their best to keep up to date with the best of the fanzines.

Sing Out, 270 Lafayette St., New York, NY 10012. An excellent, long established folk magazine. "One little issue of *Sing Out* is worth more to this humanly race than any thousand tons of other dreamy, dopey junk dished out from the trees and forests along every Broadway in this world." — *Woody Guthrie*

Living Blues, 2615 N. Wilton Ave., Chicago, IL 60614. "A Journal of the Black American Blues Tradition." Essential reading for blues fans traveling the US as it provides data on tours, festivals and radio. Excellent articles, interviews, reviews and photographs. Each Nov/Dec issue has a "Blues Radio Guide."

down beat, 222 W. Adams Street, Chicago, IL 60606 (subscription address). A long established jazz magazine though these days it labels itself "the contemporary music magazine." At the back there's a useful though rather short club listing section called "City Scene."

Pickin', North American Building, 401 N. Broad St., Philadelphia, PA 19108. "Bluegrass/country/folk/country and western/classical/jazz/old time/Dixieland fashions and lifestyles." Monthly with a strong emphasis on bluegrass and old-timey music. The October issue usually carries the annual "Guide to Bluegrass on the Radio."

Bluegrass Unlimited, Box 111, Broad Run, VA 22014. Monthly. The April issue each year contains the "Bluegrass Festival Schedule" for the summer months. Two other useful features for bluegrass fans on the move in the US are "Personal Appearance Calendar" and "Now Appearing — Bluegrass Music."

Country Music, Box 2560, Boulder, CO 80302 (subscription address). This monthly magazine calls itself "America's Number One Country Publication" though it's probably the best in the world. In-depth articles on the best of country music.

Bomp, PO Box 7112, Burbank, CA 91510. Magazine once called "Who Put The Bomp" covers pop music new and old. Very good for helping you find new rock bands on obscure labels. The magazine's obsession with English music can be seen in the remarkable on-going series "The Encyclopedia of British Rock" which attempts to compile complete information about every record made between 1962-66 that's linked to the "English Invasion."

Goldmine, PO Box 187, Frazer, MI 48026. Aimed at record collectors everywhere, there are numerous articles about obscure pop artists of the past and dozens of lists of records for sale. Fascinating reading.

Rolling Stone, Box 2983, Boulder, CO 80302. (Subscription address). Probably the most widely read music paper in the world. It travels abroad by sea and loses its freshness as the weeks pass between its publication and the time foreign readers receive it. In America, when it's more up to date, it feels and reads much better.

Among the dozens of little magazines that cover aspects of the folk, old-time music and bluegrass scenes are:

Dulcimer Player News, PO Box 157, Front Royal, VA 22630. A quarterly publication for and about the dulcimer, hammered and plucked, written for and by dulcimer people.

The Folk Life, PO Box 1041, Norristown, PA 19401. Monthly devoted to traditional music and dancing. "We bring you festival and concert information, record and book reviews and glimpses of folk life."

Mugwumps, 1600 Billman Lane, Silver Spring, MD 20902. Magazine devoted to banjos, guitars, dulcimers, harmonicas, fiddles, autoharps, tin whistles, flutes. Histories of the companies that made them, articles about how to repair, identify, date and evaluate the old ones, plans and instructions on how to build your own.

Mandolin Notebook (same address as Mugwumps, above). Bimonthly for all mandolin enthusiasts.

Banjo Newsletter, 1310 Hawkins Lane, Annapolis, MD 21401. The monthly magazine for five-string banjo enthusiasts.

Several of the most informative magazines about American music are written and produced abroad, especially in Britain.

Blues Unlimited, 36 Belmont Park, Lewisham, London SE 13 5DB, England. American agent Dick Shurman, 217 N. Lincolnway No. 224, N. Aurora, Illinois 60542. Bi-monthly devoted to the blues. Beautifully presented with lots of very atmospheric photographs, great interviews and carefully researched discographies.

Old Time Music, 33 Brunswick Gardens, London W8 4AW, England. Another well-produced magazine — it appears four times a year under the editorship of Tony Russell and contains news, interviews and discographies of old time and Western swing musicians.

Country Music People, 128a Lowfield Street, Dartford, Kent, England. Long established country music glossy magazine.

New Kommotion, 3 Bowrons Avenue, Wembley, Middlesex, England. Excellent magazine for collectors of rock 'n' roll records. Probably the best of its kind in the world.

Omaha Rainbow, 10 Lesley Court, Harcourt Road, Wallington, Surrey, England. A consistently excellent fanzine — Californian singer/songwriter John Stewart is featured in every issue. Music ranges from bluegrass through modern country to the pop sounds of sixties bands like The Mamas and the Papas.

Comstock Lode, 49 Third Cross Road, Twickenham, Middlesex, England. John Platt's little magazine has a strong penchant for the music and culture of San Francisco. Past issues have featured fascinating articles on "The Beats" and "San Francisco Poster Art."

Dark Star, 58 Islip Manor Road, Northolt, Middlesex, England. Well produced bi-monthly that focuses on the music of the US West Coast.

Manana, Ronderlin, Station Road, Newmachar, Aberdeen, Scotland. Fanzine devoted to the music of Jimmy Buffett plus modern country musicians like Michael Nesmith and Guy Clark.

Il Muchio Selvaggio, Via Val Trompia 140, 00141 Roma, Italy. Magazine with a strong interest in West Coast and modern country music. Recommended even if you don't speak Italian — production is of a very high quality.

Coast to Coast, 1-19-4, Ogawa, Machida-Shi, Tokyo 194, Japan. Covers modern country music and is entirely written in Japanese. Published three or four times a year.

Jazz, Blues & Co., 1 Rue Dallos, 75013 Paris, France. Good magazine covering jazz, blues and rock 'n' roll.

Block, Persbureau Bossa Nova, Postbus 244, 7600 AE Alamo, Netherlands. Blues magazine.

Blues Life, Steingasse 26/3/3 55, A-1030 Wenen, Austria. Blues magazine.

Country Gazette, Zwanenwater 25, 2771 KL Boskoop, Netherlands. Country music.

Dr. Jazz, Niewe achtergracht 27-huis, 1018 XW Amsterdam, Netherlands.

German Blues Circle Information, PO Box 180212, 600 Frankfurt 18, Germany.

Micography, Stevinstraat 14, 2405 CP Alphen a/d Rijn, Netherlands. Jazz magazine.

R-O-C-K, Postbox 48, Hovseter, Oslo 7, Norway. Rock 'n' roll.

Boogie Woogie & Blues Collector, Maasdrielhof 175, 1106 NG Amsterdam-zuidoost, Netherlands.

Rock & Roll International Magazine, (v/h Rockville Int), Tullipvaenget 4, 4623 Li Skensved, Denmark.

Swingtime, Bruggestraat 26, B-8080 Ruiselde, Belgium. Jazz and blues.

BOMP!

ACKNOWLEDGEMENTS

I am especially grateful for the help and encouragement I have received from Charlie Gillett, Charlie McKissack, Peter O'Brien, Barry Ballard, John Lomax, Joe Nick Patoski, Tony Paris, Steve Sagik, Mick Plumpton, David Fricke, Richard Harrington and Jon Newlin.

In addition to those thanked within the listings I am grateful to Tony Russell, Anthony Wall, Dilly Barlowe, Rachel Hodgkin, Mike Rowe, John Tobler, Fred Dellar, Hilary Hughes, Gill Gill, Roger Press, Ian Milne, Terry Andrews, John Fitzgibbon, Hope and Eric Henning, DJA, Ellen and Julie Robertson, Cliff White, Tony Byworth, Bill Sloane, Paul Slattery, Paul Beecham, Kelly DeLaney, Alan Messer, Susan Fugle, Dale Rosen, Tad Jones, Jonathan Morrish, Kristin Tregillus, Dave Walters, Sharon Wheeler, Rob Partridge, Pat Stead, Geoff Thorn, Paul Kuntab, Charlie McCutcheon, Stan Britt, Bernadette Kilmartin, Bob Fisher, Sonnie Rae, Paul Conroy, Carol Stein, Nick Kimberley, Owen Cody, Judy Totton, Keith Taylorson, David Ogden, Tony Raynor, Phil Abel, Chris Wrigley, Rod Owen, Maurice Beehan, Marris Johnson, Dianna Pugh, Dave King, Denis Lewis, Lesley and Ken Stanford, Maureen and Mac, Debbie Bennett, David Yeats, Jan Wain, Bill Moore, Wayne Asher, Alan Barton, Rod Wilson, Judith Ann Newton, Kingsley Grimble and Eric Spragett. Apologies to anyone I've left out.

I would like to acknowledge the use of the following papers and magazines in the preparation of this guide: Melody Maker, New Musical Express, Rolling Stone, Billboard, Country Music People, Omaha Rainbow, Blues Unlimited, ZigZag, Boston Phoenix, The Real Paper, Village Voice, The New York Times, SoHo News, The Aquarian, The Washington Post, Unicorn Times, The Washingtonian, The Drummer, Hank, The Tennessean, Figaro, La Gazette des Acadians, Texas Monthly, The Austin Sun, Picking Up The Tempo, Buddy, Reader, Chicago, Illinois Entertainer, Sing Out, Rocky Mountain Musical Express, Scene, Country Music, Atlanta Gazette, Living Blues, Pickin', Bluegrass Unlimited, Not Fade Away, Mother Jones, MiSC, BAM, San Francisco Bay Guardian,

Los Angeles Times, Gris Gris.

Also some books: *Vagabonding in America* by Ed Buryn, *Tripping In America* by Bill Thomas, *Amazing America* by Jane and Michael Stern, *The Moneywise Guide To North America* by Michael von Haag and Anna Crew, *The Encyclopedia of Rock* edited by Phil Hardy and Dave Laing, *National Council for the Traditional Arts Calendar of Festivals, Making Tracks* by Charlie Gillett.

NOTES

NOTES

NOTES

NOTES

NOTES

NOTES

NOTES

CORRECTIONS AND ADDITIONS

Completed slips should be sent to Richard Wootton, 21 Melbourne Court, Anerley Road, Penge, London SE 20 8AR, England.

Place: **Date:**

Subject:

Correction/Addition	**Remarks**

Place: **Date:**

Subject:

Correction/Addition	**Remarks**

Place: **Date:**

Subject:

Correction/addition	**Remarks**

CORRECTIONS AND ADDITIONS

Completed slips should be sent to Richard Wootton, 21 Melbourne Court, Anerley Road, Penge, London SE 20 8AR, England.

Place: **Date:**

Subject:

Correction/Addition	**Remarks**

Place: **Date:**

Subject:

Correction/Addition	**Remarks**

Place: **Date:**

Subject:

Correction/addition	**Remarks**

CORRECTIONS AND ADDITIONS

Completed slips should be sent to Richard Wootton, 21 Melbourne Court, Anerley Road, Penge, London SE 20 8AR, England.

Place: **Date:**

Subject:

Correction/Addition	**Remarks**

— — — — — — — — — — — —

Place: **Date:**

Subject:

Correction/Addition	**Remarks**

— — — — — — — — — — — —

Place: **Date:**

Subject:

Correction/addition	**Remarks**

CORRECTIONS AND ADDITIONS

Completed slips should be sent to Richard Wootton, 21 Melbourne Court, Anerley Road, Penge, London SE 20 8AR, England.

Place: **Date:**

Subject:

Correction/Addition	**Remarks**

Place: **Date:**

Subject:

Correction/Addition	**Remarks**

Place: **Date:**

Subject:

Correction/addition	**Remarks**

CORRECTIONS AND ADDITIONS

Please use these forms to report changes and corrections to information listed in this guide. They should also be used for returning any new information or general comments. Please give addresses and telephone numbers, make sure your information is accurate and keep your remarks short but quotable. Remember that a comment like "Quite good" or "OK" conveys little to anyone. Any further information should be sent on separate sheets of paper. Clippings from local papers that list music gigs and information are especially useful. If you send anything you want back, please enclose a self-addressed envelope.

Completed slips should be sent to Richard Wootton, 21 Melbourne Court, Anerley Road, Penge, London SE 20 8AR, England. If possible by mid-October, please.

EXAMPLE

Place: Austin, Texas **Date:** August 23

Subject: Club

Correction/Addition	Remarks
Waterloo Ice House 906 Congress (no phone)	Tiny listening room for jazz and folk bands. No cover.